CORE MANAGEMENT
PRINCIPLES

CORE MANAGEMENT
PRINCIPLES

No Flavors of the Month

D I M I T R I   P O J I D A E F F

iUniverse, Inc.
Bloomington

CORE MANAGEMENT PRINCIPLES
No Flavors of the Month

iUniverse books may be ordered through booksellers or by contacting:

iUniverse
1663 Liberty Drive
Bloomington, IN 47403
www.iuniverse.com
1-800-Authors (1-800-288-4677)

ISBN: 978-1-4759-1265-4 (sc)
ISBN: 978-1-4759-1266-1 (hc)
ISBN: 978-1-4759-1267-8 (ebk)

Library of Congress Control Number: 2012907001

Printed in the United States of America

iUniverse rev. date: 04/25/2012

DEDICATION

In Memory of Dima

for

Mary and Jason

and

with much love and thanks
to Olive for the time

PREFACE

It was over eighteen years ago, when we first established our consulting practice, that I became interested in all the various flavors of the month that were, and still are, so prevalent: Total Quality Management, Continuous Improvement, Empowerment, the list is endless. Everyone was, and still is, searching for the magic silver bullet. As a consultant, I wanted to be sure that I wasn't missing something that we could offer our clients as a ready fix for their organizational problems.

Fortunately, I already had a great deal of first-hand experience with various flavors that I had had the responsibility for implementing in my capacity as a Director of Human Resources for several large organizations in different parts of the country. All such attempts at organizational change had left me quite cynical and frustrated with an appalling lack of success in every case. I was also tired of trying to defend the use of such ineffective and bureaucratic practices as the annual performance evaluation.

Because of this interest, I sought out my old texts and purchased a few that I didn't have. I went back to some of the well-known original research in the whole area of organizational behavior and employee motivation: the research of Frederick Herzberg, Douglas McGregor, Abraham Maslow, Dr. Marrow and others. What immediately became clear, after reading their original works, was that there *are* enduring core principles of effective management, which had been clearly identified over 50 years ago. This is outlined in the first chapter, Core Principles, which is a slightly modified version of an article that was published in the *Journal for Quality and Participation*. (Pojidaeff, 1995, pp. 44-47)

Different scholars over the years have presented the principles from different viewpoints and with different terminology, but the principles have remained the same: "Employees wish to be masters of their own fate and to have a real sense of ownership. When provided with such an organizational climate, employees are able to use their own intrinsic motivation to improve productivity and maintain high quality and good service."

What also became so abundantly clear was that most of the flavors of the month were valid programs; the reason that they so quickly became the latest flavor of the month, however, was, in most cases, because the core principles were neglected in their implementation. A common example is the attempt to implement Total Quality Management or Continuous Improvement without a participative management culture in which full responsibility and accountability is delegated to the individual employee.

Since that time, many books, many articles, and many clients later, this book has been slowly developing. It is my very strong bias, and that of my partners, that the management of people is the most critical aspect of good management and productive organizations. Sales, marketing, finance, systems, engineering, production, and all other areas of any organization, are developed by people, operated by people, and managed by people. No matter what the technology, it is still also developed and operated by people. People are the only sustainable competitive advantage.

This statement itself has, unfortunately, become one of the worst flavors of the month as most managers only pay lip service, at best, to it. There is too much evidence, however, as will be shown, to ignore the primary importance of our human resources to the overall productivity of any organization.

Yet the management of people is the least taught management skill. There is some growing recognition of this problem, but the required change in the curricula of our business education programs is far too slow. The focus is still on finance, marketing, sales, and the other traditional business courses. The same holds true for the public sector as well, where the emphasis is on such areas as legislation, policy, and public finance.

The intent of this book is to fill this need in some small measure by providing a simple, straightforward account of what the appropriate and practical people management and organizational skills are to create and sustain a productive workplace, from the time of hiring a new employee through to possible termination and the steps in between. It is true that good managers today must be leaders. Good leaders, however, must understand and ensure productive people management and organizational practices in order to lead.

The core principles are strong and enduring. With every new client we realize how firmly our practice is based on these principles. When in doubt about how to deal with a certain issue, we only have to refer back to them to help guide both our clients and us. The core principles have never let us down. We have never had to resort to any "flavor of the month".

My thanks to all those scholars, past and present, whose work is reflected and referred to in this book. Thanks also to past employers and all our clients, who have contributed to the practical experience and knowledge that I have attempted to outline in this book. And finally, thanks to my partners for their many years of support, collaboration, good humor, and helpful criticism.

Dimitri Pojidaeff
February, 2012

CONTENTS

PREFACE..vii

CHAPTER I—CORE PRINCIPLES 1

New developments or flavors of the month? 1
Intrinsic motivation 2
Three classic motivation theories................................. 2
The birth of participative management........................... 4
Why the interest in such old concepts? 5
Why the continued resistance to proven principles?........... 5
The machine model organization 6
Misunderstanding power and control 7
New labels, old system 7
Today's organizational paradox 8

CHAPTER II—PRODUCTIVE WORKPLACES 9

Core competencies 9
Productive Workplace Behaviors 11
The great paradox.. 12
Organizational Inhibitors... 12
Accountability and democracy................................... 13
Bureaucracy and productivity.................................... 14
Productive organizational practices............................. 14

CHAPTER III—MANAGEMENT STYLE—LETTING GO 19

Theory of Job Enrichment.. 20
Participative management 21
Accountability for results... 22
Information and responsibility................................... 22
Solving problems that belong to others......................... 23
Fair rewards.. 23

Letting go...23
Middle management will disappear....................................24
Management training...25

CHAPTER IV—START RIGHT; HIRE RIGHT!..............27

Avoid significant grief! Get it right in the first place!......27
Manage your primary risk..28
Competencies and behaviors...29
Always check references. 31
The best references are usually the informal ones 32
A time consuming process 34

CHAPTER V—STAFF DEVELOPMENT............................35

Keep training at all times..36
Jobs vs Work..36
Types of staff development..37

CHAPTER VI—MANAGING PERFORMANCE...............41

What is performance management? 41
Traditional performance evaluation 42
Performance must be managed as and when required......42
Productive review of performance....................................43
Performance management is supportive, but firm. 44
Avoiding performance issues...45
Why performance issues must be addressed. 47

CHAPTER VII—PRODUCTIVE TERMINATION...........49

Termination can and should be productive for all concerned.......49
Excuses for avoiding the issue...50
The employees concerned are harmed. 50
Ignoring the problem severely affects other staff. 51
The organization as a whole suffers. 51
The earlier the better. 51

CHAPTER VIII—ORGANIZATIONAL STRUCTURE FLATTER IS BETTER 53

Increase in organizational democracy 53
The Redundancy Hierarchy Test 54
Why keep the traditional hierarchical
        organizational structure? 55
Traditional organizational structure and management style........56
Flatter is better 58
Change the structure and change the culture 58

CHAPTER IX—CONTROL—WHO'S IN CHARGE?....................59

Everyone shares in the overall control of the organization............59
Bureaucracy..60
Policies 60
Mutual trust and respect and the use of discretion........................62
Rules and Regulations...62
Job Descriptions..63
Performance evaluation 64
Customer service 65
"Just Do It!" 65

CHAPTER X—REWARDS...67

Lack of alignment 67
Traditional views 68
The giant mismatch..69
"The things that get rewarded get done." 69
Pay raises based on performance evaluation 70
Ownership..71
Open-book management..72
Pay for competencies, not the job..72

CHAPTER XI—CHECK YOUR ALIGNMENT 73

The Paradox 73
Organizational Inhibitors 73

A system's perspective 74
What is alignment? 75
The equal treatment of unequals 77

CHAPTER XII—QUANTITATIVE VERSUS QUALITATIVE 79

What gets measured, gets managed 79
Metrics a useful aid 79
Reliance on metrics 80
Metrics not a substitute for judgement and discretion 80

CHAPTER XIII—UNDERCOVER BOSS 84

Personal knowledge, not just performance data 84
It is not a question of trust, but rather common sense. 86
The manager is ultimately responsible. 86

CHAPTER XIV—WHY MANAGERS GET FIRED 87

Technical competence 87
Today's competencies 88
Required competencies least taught 89
The main reasons why managers get fired 90
Failure to deal with performance issues 90
Management's primary responsibility 92

CHAPTER XV—GOOD MANAGEMENT IS LEADERSHIP 93

Leadership the latest flavor of the month 93
Leadership distinct from management? 93
One cannot be a good manager without being a leader. 95
Leaders, on the other hand, must be good managers. 95
Core Principles, not silver bullets 96

REFERENCES 97

ABOUT THE AUTHOR 99

Chapter 1

CORE PRINCIPLES

New developments or flavors of the month?

If the number of buzzwords is any indication, there have been many supposedly new developments over the past decade or so in the field of Human Resources Management and Organizational Development: Empowerment, Teamwork, Quality Management, Continuous Improvement, Participative Management, Reengineering, Restructuring, and, of course, let's not forget, Excellence. It is no wonder, therefore, that Peter Senge (1992, pp.30-38), author of *The Fifth Discipline: The Art and Practice of the Learning Organization*, had this to say:

> . . . the quality movement . . . risks being fragmented into isolated initiatives and slogans. The voice of the customer, fix the process not the people, competitive benchmarking, continuous improvement, policy deployment, leadership—the more we hear, the less we understand.

> It is not surprising that, for many, it doesn't add up to much more than management's latest flavor of the month that must be endured until the next fad comes along.

So how do we, or can we, make any sense out of all this theory and literature that we're being inundated with? Does any of it actually work? Is it all just a fad? Where does it all originate? The answer to all these questions is the old French expression, *Plus ça change, plus c'est la même chose.* The more things change, the more they remain the same.

Intrinsic motivation

They remain the same, because all of these supposedly new theories primarily involve the core principle of transforming management practices and reforming workplaces so that employees can utilize their own intrinsic motivation to learn, to achieve, to gain esteem, to improve, to look for better ways of doing things and in the process, of course, to improve productivity and maintain consistently high quality and service.

Three classic motivation theories

Three classic, traditional theories of human motivation have provided most of the basis of human resource management theory for the past four to five decades:

1. **Abraham Maslow** (1987) first described his theory of a hierarchy of needs in his book, *Motivation and Personality,* which was first published in 1954. That's 58 years ago! The top of his hierarchy of motivational factors was what he called self-actualization or the desire to become everything that one is capable of becoming; to make the very most of one's potential. Esteem needs were ranked second. Both self-actualization and esteem, of course, can only be realized in a participative workplace, which fosters intrinsic motivation through empowerment, responsibility, and a real sense of ownership. This is the same principle that underlies all current theories of quality management.
2. **Frederick Herzberg** (1966) wrote *Work and the Nature of Man* in 1966, 46 years ago. In that book he put forth his theory of Maintenance versus Motivation factors and the concept of Job Enrichment. Maintenance factors are *extrinsic* to the job and include such things as working conditions, salary, and company policies. Motivation factors, on the other hand, are *intrinsic* to

the job, and include such things as achievement, recognition, responsibility, growth, and the work itself.

Twenty-six years later, Peter Senge (1992, pp.30-38) writes:

"The prevailing system of management has destroyed our people," says Dr. Deming. "People are born with intrinsic motivation, self-esteem, dignity, curiosity to learn, joy in learning."

Intrinsic motivation lies at the heart of Deming's management philosophy. By contrast, extrinsic motivation is the bread and butter of Western management.

. . . A corporate commitment to quality that is not based on intrinsic motivation is a house built on sand.

3. **Douglas McGregor** (1960) presented his ideas of Theory X and Theory Y in *The Human Side of Enterprise*, which was published 52 years ago in 1960. Management's beliefs about human behavior, according to McGregor, lead to those management concepts, practices, and procedures that foster and support that same behavior. They are to a great extent, in effect, self-fulfilling beliefs. A Theory X view of human behavior holds that employees dislike work and responsibility, prefer to be led, and must be forced to do a good job. Theory Y, on the other hand, states that employees seek responsibility, want to be productive, want to achieve, and are capable of problem solving. Theory X, of course, leads to the use of *extrinsic* motivators, which maintain Theory X behavior and do nothing to promote Theory Y behavior. Theory Y, however, promotes the use of *intrinsic* motivators, which in turn foster the continuation of Theory Y behavior. In the preface, McGregor (1960, p.vi) writes:

Without in the least minimizing the importance of the work that has been done to improve the selection of people with managerial potential, I have come to the conviction that some of our most important problems lie elsewhere.

> Even if we possessed methods enabling us to do a perfect job of selecting young men with the capacity to become top executives, the practical gain for industry would be negligible under today's conditions. The reason is that we have not learned enough about the utilization of talent, about the creation of an organizational climate conducive to human growth. The blunt fact is that we are a long way from realizing the potential represented by the human resources we now recruit into industry.

The core principles, no matter what past or current buzzword we use to describe them, remain the same. Employees wish to be masters of their own fate and to have a real sense of ownership. When provided with such an organizational climate, employees are able to use their own intrinsic motivation to improve productivity and maintain high quality and good service.

The birth of participative management

Dr. Alfred J. Marrow (1969) is known as the father of participative management. In 1947, 65 years ago, he was C.E.O. of an apparel manufacturing company called Harwood. The workforce was comprised of poorly educated young women from the rural mountain areas around the plant. Productivity was low in general and dropped by as much as 25% every time a change was introduced. As a psychologist, Dr. Marrow was interested in the causes of this behavior and how to change it. He and his colleagues found that productivity consistently increased by as much as 14% when employees were allowed to make meaningful decisions concerning their own work; in other words, participative management dramatically and quickly increased productivity. Dr. Marrow wrote, "The problem is the 25-year time lag between discovery of new evidence and its general application. This gap has occurred because the present generation of executives has been unwilling to replace dying managerial traditions and to start learning a new system."

Why the interest in such old concepts?

It's now 65 years later. Aside from Dr. Marrow's underestimated 25-year time lag, what has changed to explain the immense interest in such old concepts? The economic climate has. The global economy and ever increasing freer trade means that our businesses must be competitive or perish. There are no longer any alternatives; our businesses must become more productive. Both the private and increasingly the public sector have tried many possible means of reducing costs and increasing productivity: just-in-time inventory, improved cost controls, more consistent quality control, robotics, and changes in product design and service delivery to name only a few. Once these systemic means have been exhausted, however, we have only one means left—our human resources. Many organizations have first tried to reduce their human resource costs by downsizing and cutbacks in pay. Past a certain point, however, this approach cannot continue if a certain level of service and production is to be maintained. The only competitive advantage then left is in human productivity and creating an organizational climate that supports and enhances it.

Why the continued resistance to proven principles?

It is gratifying to finally see such interest in our human resources, even if it is forced purely by the need to improve the bottom line. On the other hand, it is so very frustrating that we are still discussing the same core principles over half a century later. If they have lasted for this long, they must obviously be well rooted and accepted as valid. Why haven't we fully embraced them and absorbed them into our organizational cultures? Why are we still so resistant to changes that we admit will be of benefit to us? Why has, according to Peter Senge (1992, pp.30-38), extrinsic motivation been the bread and butter of Western management?

The machine model organization

The reasons are simple, but firmly entrenched. In order to manage the diversity and complexity of both big business and big government, we abandoned the core principles in favor of those practices that minimize the idiosyncrasies of human behavior. This was achieved by focusing on the organizational elements of strategy, structure, and systems. These elements, believed to be essential to providing focus and control, have evolved into highly complex processes exerting a great impact on our human resources by increasing the degree of fragmentation and systematization of work processes. In most organizations this has lead to the implicit view by management that people are merely replaceable spokes in the business cycle and has created jobs that are narrowly defined, mundane, and devoid of meaning to the people who perform them.

This has been the fundamental basis of the bureaucratic, hierarchical organization; a structure that breeds rigidity, poor communication, and slow response, and stifles any intrinsic motivation. According to Gary Hamel and C.K. Prahalad (1989, p.75):

> In this hierarchy, senior management makes strategy and lower levels execute it. But the strategy hierarchy undermines competitiveness by fostering an elitist view of management that tends to disenfranchise most of the organization. Employees fail to identify with corporate goals and involve themselves deeply in the work of becoming more competitive.

This approach is also reflective of our culture. Government in its wisdom has known best what the needs of its constituents are and has provided program after program to take care of those needs from "cradle to grave." With a diminishing ability to raise taxes and the burden of immense debt, however, government is now forced to dismantle many of these programs and move back to a more participative democracy where people are encouraged to make their own contributions to meet their needs.

After so many years of the strategy, structure, and systems approach, as well as having the same approach taught in virtually every school of business, it is quite understandable that there is such widespread resistance to any change that requires giving up control and implementing a more participative workplace, which supports intrinsic motivation. Yet this is precisely what must be done to ensure continued prosperity with fewer opportunities to achieve competitive advantage.

Misunderstanding power and control

Most managers and supervisors, however, are fearful of change that breaks down hierarchical structures, empowers workers, and disperses control. They perceive a loss of power, control, prestige, and esteem because they misunderstand the concepts of participation and empowerment. They consider them a threat to their traditional roles as well as a threat to their job security. Such perceptions lead to very strong resistance and, in some cases, sabotage of any change process. Giving up power and control is a very difficult transition for management. It defies their entire training and experience as well as our very culture. Managers have been taught for years that they must *manage* staff, that they must provide goals, direction, and motivation and that they must, therefore, *control* others.

Many organizations recognize the need for change, but are reluctant and afraid to implement the core principles and provide a truly participative work environment. As a result, they do not engage the whole organization in the change process, thereby failing to create intrinsic individual commitment to the outcome. The process is still being managed and controlled at the top. Only when everyone is deeply engaged in and responsible for change is it going to be successful. Pretense of total participation throughout the organization only results in cynicism, poor motivation, and decreased productivity.

New labels, old system

Other organizations insist that they truly desire a more participative workplace and have adopted such a strategy, but they leave the same structures and systems in place that support continued extrinsic control. For a truly participative workplace to survive, strategy, structure, and all systems must be supportive. Re-labeling a supervisor as a "team leader", for example, does not change the location of responsibility for control and coordination of work. The power structure remains unchanged. Appraisal and reward systems that continue to reflect typical hierarchical, fragmented, and competitive roles are also at odds with a truly participative workplace.

Today's organizational paradox

These change efforts attempt to create a more democratic workplace, but continue to use processes, structures, and governance that are bureaucratic; this is the paradox inherent in so many of today's organizations. Because these efforts, therefore, are never truly successful, many organizations continually move from one attempt to the next and create the unfortunate "flavor of the month" syndrome which is costly, time consuming, and counterproductive to the desired increase in productivity.

These then are the reasons why the core principles are still not fully embraced by and absorbed into our organizational cultures. It is easy, under the circumstances, to be cynical about the endless parade of buzzwords, supposedly new theories and change processes and many are, especially those subjected to the endless parade of flavors of the month. We cannot let this obscure, however, the validity of the core principles; without them nothing really changes or succeeds over time. Those organizations, both private and public, that do not adopt them will no longer survive. The lack of a participative workplace to support intrinsic motivation is the major reason for the lack of competitive advantage in the private sector and the staggering cost of our bloated bureaucracies in the public sector.

**A return to the core principles is a return
to the fundamental beliefs of our North American
heritage: individual responsibility with minimal
democratic governance.**

Chapter II

PRODUCTIVE WORKPLACES

"They copied all they could,
but they couldn't copy my mind;
and I left them sweating and stealing,
a year and a half behind."

—Rudyard Kipling

The need for competitive advantage has finally focused the attention of many organizations and their leaders on the potential productivity of their human resources. People and their minds are the only sustainable competitive advantage:

**All aspects of any organization are conducted
by its human resources and all technological and systemic
advances are soon copied or bettered.
The only real and sustainable competitive advantage,
therefore, is through your human resources.**

Core competencies

An organization's ability to become more productive, cost effective, innovative, and adaptable to change is dependent upon the core competencies of all its employees. Organizations are now demanding from their employees, therefore, those competencies and behaviors that foster and support those organizational attributes that create competitive advantage:

- **Customer Service:** Determining and satisfying the needs of both internal and external customers must be the focus of everyone throughout the organization. In the past all that mattered was satisfying the boss.
- **Focus on the work:** Narrowly focused jobs and the traditional job description prevent an awareness of the overall work that needs to be accomplished and lead to the "It's not in my job description!" syndrome.
- **Ownership:** Employees at all levels must assume ownership of the work that they do, the quality of that work, and the day-to-day decisions surrounding their work. Responsibility for work must be delegated to the level at which the work is actually done.
- **Teamwork:** If we need employees to be aware of the overall work that needs to be accomplished and to assume ownership of it, then they also need to work together as a team to ensure that there is mutual understanding of and cooperation in attaining corporate goals.
- **Knowledge and Creativity:** We need employees with expertise and knowledge that is relevant and up-to-date. We need creativity rather than the traditional subservient compliance that is so prevalent in our bureaucracies. We need an organizational culture that fosters continuous learning and allows for mistakes. Remember that 3M's Post-it Note was the result of a *poor* batch of glue!
- **Initiative:** We need initiative rather than strict adherence to accepted practice and procedure and fear of taking ownership. This fear is so evident in those large bureaucracies that have a multitude of hierarchical layers and committees behind which everyone can hide and avoid taking responsibility.
- **Entrepreneurship:** According to Tom Peters, everyone had best achieve the mind-set of an independent contractor. Many organizations are finding it more productive and cost effective to outsource many of their functions to outside contractors. They are also treating many of their inside staff functions as if they were independent contractors and insisting that they

pay their own way by selling their services to the rest of the organization.

- **Problem Resolution:** In the past we required employees to "park their brains" at the plant gate and to dutifully refer all problems up the line. We now require everyone's expertise in order to resolve problems and who better to try and resolve them than those actually doing the work?
- **Continuous Improvement:** Tradition and consistency must now be replaced with continuous improvement. Employees must constantly look for ways of improving processes, procedures, products, and services.
- **Cross-functional:** We require employees who can work in a cross-functional environment. Organizations cannot survive with the traditional silo mentality where, for example, production and maintenance don't cooperate and sales, marketing, and finance all vie for control. This necessity is coupled with the demand for employees who are multi-skilled, so that they have a better appreciation for the broader picture, so that they have greater problem solving knowledge, and so that the organization has far greater flexibility in manpower planning.

TABLE 1
PRODUCTIVE WORKPLACE BEHAVIORS

Traditional behaviors	Productive behaviors
Serve the boss	Serve the customer
Do the *job*	Focus on the *work*
Refer "up the ladder"	Ownership
Do your own job	Teamwork
Conformity	Knowledge and creativity
Blind adherence to policies/rules	Initiative
Seniority	Entrepreneurship/add value
Problem referral	Problem resolution
Tradition/consistency	Continuous improvement
Specialized work	Cross-functional/multi-skilled

Table 1 shows these productive competencies against the traditional ones. These competencies are, of course, highly interrelated and are not by any means all-inclusive, but represent some of the most important. It should be noted that they are desired at all levels of the organization and have been missing at all levels. These are not competencies that have been lacking and suppressed purely at the blue collar and lower levels of an organization; they have been equally missing from the management ranks including executive and professional offices. This is not peculiar to any one segment of our economy; it is true for both the private and public sector, the service and manufacturing industries, the academic institution, and the research laboratory.

The great paradox

Most of our organizations need these competencies and behaviors, yet they continue with traditional practices, structures, and systems, which inhibit them and prevent their success. This is the inherent paradox within these organizations and the fundamental reason for the failure of so many change processes and the resultant frustration and cynicism of employees regarding the latest "flavor of the month." Table 2 illustrates these organizational inhibitors:

TABLE 2
ORGANIZATIONAL INHIBITORS

Productive Behaviors	Organizational inhibitors
Customer service	Volume/cost focus
Focus on the *work*	Rigid, narrow *job* descriptions
Ownership	Lack of delegation
Teamwork	Focus on the individual
Knowledge and creativity	Rigid policies/rules
Initiative	Control orientation
Entrepreneurship	Paternal/authoritarian
Problem resolution	Multi-level hierarchy
Continuous improvement	Set, established methods
Cross-functional/multi-skilled	Functional specialization

- How can one expect all employees to focus on providing excellent customer service when the corporate focus is on volume of production, cost of production, and the next quarter's profit margin to the exclusion of all else? So many organizations are still only willing to change their management practices when their output of production is actually threatened; when they have their backs to the wall and are fighting for their very survival.

- Persuading employees to focus on the broader picture of the overall work that needs to be done is virtually impossible when their jobs are still narrowly defined, when multi-skilling is not encouraged or rewarded, and when employees are subject to numerous bureaucratic policies and procedures that attempt to govern all behavior.

- Employees cannot take ownership of their work unless the responsibility is fully delegated to them and many of the traditional bureaucratic controls are removed. One cannot have personal accountability without the delegation of responsibility.

**There is far greater individual accountability
in a democratic and participative workplace than
there is in a bureaucratic workplace that attempts
to control all behavior.**

- Many organizations are insisting on teamwork, yet they still adhere to their traditional narrow job descriptions, they still retain the same hierarchical structure, they still appraise individual performance, and they still reward individual performance rather than team and organizational performance.

- How can we expect creativity, a desire for knowledge, individual initiative and entrepreneurship, and continuous improvement in the midst of a stifling, traditional, authoritarian organizational culture with numerous rules and procedures and little if any delegation of responsibility?

- Employees cannot and will not resolve their own work problems unless the responsibility is delegated to them, unless they are given the necessary access to required information and tools, and unless the traditional hierarchical levels which encourage referral "up the line" are removed.

- Cross-functionality together with multi-skilling is highly desirable for increased flexibility in manpower usage, better and more accurate communications, greater problem solving capabilities, and better organizational teamwork. This cannot occur unless the organizational structure itself is changed to reflect the desired mix of functions. There is no point in hiring or developing multi-skilled employees unless the organizational structure and culture will allow them to function.

> **You cannot create a productive and participative workplace, when bureaucratic structures and systems of governance remain in place.**

When we examine these organizational inhibitors in light of the core principles of a productive workplace, it is easy to see that they accurately follow McGregor's Theory X view of human nature and run contrary to the principles of Herzberg's research regarding those factors that provide intrinsic motivation. They support the belief that employees dislike work, lack ambition, are not very bright, and dislike responsibility. They support the resulting principle that employees must be closely controlled, which in turn leads to highly standardized jobs, numerous rules, policies and procedures, as well as close supervision with little if any delegation of responsibility. The employees in turn do not exhibit the desired competencies and become cynical and frustrated because of the mixed messages that result from the paradox. On the one hand they're encouraged to show initiative, accept responsibility and take ownership, but on the other hand they're prevented from doing so.

Productive organizational practices

Productive organizations have learned that there is no quick fix; that the flavor of the month does not work. They have learned that strategy, structure, and systems must also be changed in order to support rather than inhibit the desired employee competencies. They have avoided the paradox by changing all aspects of the organization that inhibit or prevent the core principles of intrinsic motivation and a participative workplace:

- **The least hierarchical levels possible.** Reducing management and supervisory layers is not just a cost saving measure. It assures a much faster and more accurate flow of information in all directions, which in turn leads to faster and better decision making and a greater sharing of information throughout the organization. The less the levels the greater the delegation of responsibility to those actually doing the work and less opportunity for referring problems up the line and avoiding ownership and accountability.
- **A participative environment.** Many organizations just pay lip service to this fundamental principle. Productive ones openly share information and actively involve all employees in workplace decisions. This subject will be discussed in detail in the following chapter.
- **Delegation of responsibility.** Responsibility is fully delegated to the level at which the work is done, to the level with the actual work expertise, and the level best qualified to resolve everyday work problems, ensure quality, and provide customer service.
- **Common sense.** Rigid rules, regulations, policies, and procedures are replaced wherever possible with plain common sense. I am reminded of a client who wanted to know whether or not they could discipline an employee for demonstrably poor performance. When asked why on earth not, they replied, "Because we don't have a policy!"
- **Flexible work.** Productive organizations have ceased to continually define and fill positions to complete new work and new projects. They look at the competencies of existing staff and assign new responsibilities and projects to them. Many employees now rotate from one project to the next based on their individual competencies. This saves the organization the cost of ever-increasing bureaucracies and provides employees with a far more stimulating and challenging career.
- **A team focus.** The focus is on cooperation and teamwork and includes team based performance assessment and team based

rewards. Teams are actually self-managed and not just a group of employees with a traditional supervisor relabeled a "team leader".

- **Reward for performance.** Successful organizations reward employees for team and organizational performance, not seniority. They reward employees for their competencies and their knowledge and not just their *job* duties. They frequently have gainsharing and other reward programs, which allow all employees to have a stake in the organizational performance.

- **Cross-functional/multi-skilled.** The entire structure of these organizations has been changed to eradicate the traditional, functional, stand-alone silo. Cross-functional teams make decisions and many positions have cross-functional responsibilities. Employees are encouraged to be multi-skilled and are paid accordingly.

- **A quality/service focus.** The emphasis is on quality and customer service with the realization that this is the only means of ensuring volume and profit. If you now have to say that "Quality is Job #1", then this says everything to explain the lack of attention previously paid to quality and the reasons for the dominance of Japanese and other imports that are so popular because of their quality and reliability.

- **A learning organization.** Staff training and development is not just a collection of isolated seminars and workshops, but rather a clearly thought out developmental program for all employees that is aligned with desired competencies and overall business goals. Continuous learning is encouraged and funded and not the first budget item to be cut when profits are down. Experimentation and creativity are encouraged with the understanding that errors will occur, but that learning will result from those errors.

- **Competencies and behaviors.** The focus is on competencies and behaviors and not just skills and experience. Employees are increasingly being selected and promoted for their overall competencies and interpersonal behaviors.

- **Interest-based labor relations.** Many organizations continually use the excuse that they are unionized to explain why they have not implemented some of these best practices. Productive organizations have taken the initiative to involve their unions, to provide them with information and an opportunity to fully participate in future plans recognizing the interests of all concerned.

TABLE 3
PRODUCTIVE ORGANIZATIONAL PRACTICES

Traditional	Productive
Multi-level hierarchy	Least levels possible
Authoritarian/paternal	Participative
Control oriented	Delegated responsibility
Rules and policies	Common sense
Defined *jobs*	Flexible *work*
Individual focus	Team focus
Reward seniority	Reward performance
Functional specialization	Cross-functional
Volume/cost focus	Quality/service focus
Consistency/traditional	Learning organization
Knowledge and experience	Competencies and behaviors
Win/lose labor relations	Interest-based

Summary

We have seen what the core principles are that sustain motivation and productivity, and what the employee competencies and behaviors are that are based on these principles and are required to create a productive workplace and maintain competitive advantage. We have seen what the traditional organizational inhibitors are that prevent these competencies and behaviors, and what the best practices are of those organizations that are successful in today's economy.

The remaining chapters are devoted to the human resource management practices and principles of organizational effectiveness that foster the desired employee competencies and behaviors. The emphasis is on the management of people rather than on the management of strategy, structure, and systems, because people determine the latter and because people are the only sustainable competitive advantage.

Management's primary responsibility, therefore, is:
To provide an organizational culture where
the human resources
are motivated to
optimum productivity.

Chapter III

MANAGEMENT STYLE—LETTING GO

"Organizational performance depends on employees
caring about the work they do, knowing how to do it,
and doing the right things. Involving individuals in
the business is the most effective way to produce an
organization in which people know more, care more, and
do the right things."

—Edward E. Lawler III (1992, p.347)

The core principles of a productive workplace, as we have seen, involve intrinsic motivation or self-motivation. This, after all, is what drives entrepreneurs, inventors, scientists, great athletes, and all those who achieve greatness in their chosen field; they love the work that they do and the opportunity to achieve within the field of work that they love is all the motivation they need.

Herzberg's (1966) research, among others, showed that the factors that truly create intrinsic motivation must come from the actual work that people do. This cannot occur, therefore, if people do not find their work rewarding in the same sense that the entrepreneur, for example, does. Herzberg, as a result, put forward his theory of Job Enrichment. If the work has to be meaningful, then how do we make it so for the average employee who does not own his or her own business?

Herzberg identified five main means of enriching jobs to make the work more meaningful:

Theory of Job Enrichment

1. Remove some controls.
2. Increase personal accountability.
3. Provide timely performance information.
4. Delegate additional authority.
5. Provide complete units of work.

> **"If you want someone to do a good job,
> give them a good job to do."**
>
> —Frederick Herzberg

Many years later, we have virtually the same advice from Edward Lawler III (1986), one of today's most prominent scholars in management literature. Lawler says that the ultimate advantage for organizational effectiveness is to create a "high-involvement organization"; one that fully involves all employees at all levels. In order to accomplish this, Lawler says that information, knowledge, power, and rewards must be spread throughout the organization and not just hoarded and jealously guarded at the top levels.

Herzberg talks about providing employees with timely performance information. Lawler expands this to include not only information regarding personal performance, but also information regarding corporate performance in general. Herzberg says that one has to remove some controls and delegate additional authority, whereas Lawler talks about distributing power more evenly throughout the organization. Lawler says that rewards should also be distributed more evenly and Herzberg says that personal accountability must be increased. We can assume that with increased authority and accountability there are increased rewards. Finally Lawler recommends increasing everyone's knowledge; this is an inherent part of all of Herzberg's recommendations.

Participative management

These factors are some of the key components of what is commonly referred to as a participative management style. They cannot and will not occur under a traditional management style that believes that all aspects of an employee's work must be controlled. They necessitate full employee involvement, which in turn necessitates that management let go this traditional all encompassing control. This is easier said than done. Productive organizations, as we have seen in the preceding chapter, recognize the need for a participative approach, yet the lack of one is probably the biggest single impediment in most organizations to a productive workplace. Taking the factors, then, that have been identified by Herzberg and Lawler, we can examine in greater detail just what is involved in a participative management style.

Responsibility must be delegated to the level at which the work is actually done. It is not the lead hand, the team leader, the supervisor, or any manager that should be held responsible for the individual work of any employee; only the employee should be held responsible. After all it is the employee who actually performs the work. This sounds so obvious, yet in most organizations this does not fully occur. The full responsibility has not been delegated; there are still numerous controls for which the lead hand or some other higher level is responsible and over which the employee has no control. If responsibility is truly delegated, then the controls have to be removed and the employee has to have the authority to act. If not, we have the classic situation of passing the blame on to someone else. "It's not my responsibility; I was just following orders." "I can't help it if it didn't work; I was only following policy." "How was I supposed to know; I'm not given that information." "Don't blame me; I'm not authorized to make that kind of decision." The list of such responses is endless. One simply cannot successfully delegate responsibility without also delegating the authority.

Everyone wants to hold the employee accountable, but this is not possible unless the employee is given full responsibility and authority. This is the ironic situation in so many organizations; they try to control every aspect of employee behavior and hold employees responsible and accountable at the same time. The only thing you can reasonably hold an employee accountable for in such a situation is blind obedience, regardless of whether there are issues of customer service, quality, safety, or productivity.

Accountability for results is essential.
Employees must have full responsibility for those things
for which they are held accountable.

Delegating full responsibility means delegating the authority and removing the controls. If the work itself has to be meaningful in order to provide intrinsic motivation, then one has to have control over the work. This in turn requires full delegation of responsibility and authority, which provides ownership and, therefore, accountability. The equation is straightforward and there are no short cuts. If you don't remove the controls, then you have the paradox referred to earlier of trying to create a productive workplace with self-motivated employees, while inhibiting it at the same time with bureaucratic structures and controls. According to C.R. Farquhar and J.A. Longair (1966, p.3):

"When people believe that they can influence outcomes,
they are far more willing to be accountable for results."

Delegation also requires that employees are provided the knowledge and information required to act responsibly. If proper training and information is not provided, the employee is being set up for failure and the organization, typically, reverts back to a controlling style of management. One trend today is towards greater openness and transparency in corporate management. John Case (1995, pp.37-38) says in *Open-Book Management* that, "Every employee in an open-book company sees—and learns to understand—the company's financials, along with all other numbers that are critical to tracking the business's performance . . . . Employees assume that, whatever else they do, part of their job is to move those numbers in the right direction . . . . Employees have a direct stake in the company's success." As Blanchard, Carlos, and Randolph (1996, p.34) say:

"People without information cannot act responsibly.
People with information are compelled to act
responsibly."

When full responsibility and authority is delegated, then so is the responsibility for resolving problems. Instead of passing the buck up the line, employees are expected to make decisions and resolve most issues. Those actually doing the work are best qualified to resolve daily work problems, ensure quality, and provide customer service. If you want accountability, then employees must have ownership of problems as well. Peter Block (1993, p.72) says:

> **"It is a misuse of our power to take responsibility**
> **for solving problems that belong to others."**

Participative management also requires, as Lawler (1986) points out, that rewards be shared equitably throughout the organization. The behavior you reward is the behavior you get. The obvious inequities in most organizational compensation plans send a very clear message to most employees: It doesn't pay to really work hard, take risks and show initiative, as you will not get paid more than the next person and all of the gravy goes to the boss anyway. The immense management salaries today, coupled with the obscene "golden parachutes" in spite of irresponsible management behavior, only further increases the cynicism of a large part of today's workforce. There are obvious reasons for paying people more the higher their position in the organization, but the compensation has to be perceived as equitable and must be based on performance. This is why many productive organizations have implemented some form of true profit sharing. This is, after all, a logical extension of our free market capitalist philosophy as well as the entrepreneurial spirit. Farquhar and Longair (1966, p.15) say that:

> **"Employees take ownership for results when recognition,**
> **status and compensation are based on their performance**
> **and their contribution**
> **to the success of the organization."**

Letting go

There are no shortcuts to a truly participative management style. Managers have to let go. One of the biggest impediments to the success of participative management and a productive workplace is the partial implementation of such a management style rather than full implementation. Participation is not a matter of convening a "team" meeting to review and provide polite input to decisions that have already been made at higher levels. Participation means full delegation of responsibility for formulating solutions from the ground up. Participation means implementing all of the factors discussed above; one cannot just implement some of them. All aspects of the organization must be in tune with the core principles. This is what is referred to as "alignment" and will be discussed further in a later chapter.

Participative management requires that managers give up the traditional management style of controlling the way people work; controlling what they do, how they do it, and every other aspect of their work. Productive organizations today understand that a more democratic management style is more productive and that the traditional style is no longer accepted by most employees, especially a better educated and younger workforce. Today we talk about self managed teams, delegated responsibility and authority, empowerment, and the rise of organizational democracy in general.

The traditional management position that did most of the controlling is being removed from many organizations. Experts such as Peter Block (1993, p.66) said over 18 years ago that:

> **"No one should be able to make a living simply planning, watching, controlling, or evaluating the actions of others."**

Michael Hammer (1993, pp.51-53), the reengineering expert, said that:

> **"Middle management, as we currently know it, will simply disappear."**

Managers, of course, are still here today, but their role has significantly changed and sometimes their title. They are expected to be coaches, mentors, trainers, and facilitators who support rather than control and who are just as likely to be called team leader as manager or supervisor. They are expected to be leaders rather than controllers.

This change is strongly resisted by many managers who perceive participative management as a loss of their control, power, status, and possibly their job. It is impossible, however, to fully control all aspects of employee behavior. It is also, as stated earlier, counter productive as it prevents precisely the employee behaviors that organizations need to survive and prosper. Managers actually have far greater control and power if they ensure that employees are knowledgeable, responsible, and accountable. Managers do, however, as we see later, have to fear for their jobs—if they are unwilling to change their management style.

Management training

Our schools of management, both undergraduate and graduate, are greatly to blame for the continued resistance to a more participative and productive workplace. They continue to teach that the role of the manager is to control all aspects of business including the human resources. There are few courses that are available in human resources management, organizational development, and organizational effectiveness and few programs allow the student to major in these areas. For the most part it is the traditional courses in accounting, marketing, sales, business law, and the like, which constitute by far the majority of the curriculum. Yet we are constantly reminded that it is leaders of people that we need most.

Jeffrey Pfeffer, noted author and professor of organizational behavior at the Graduate School of Business at Stanford University, and Christina Fong (2002), a PhD candidate at Stanford, published their research into the value and relevance of an MBA degree as well as the worth of the research done at various business schools. They find that: "There is little evidence that mastery of the knowledge acquired in business schools enhances people's careers, or that even attaining the MBA credential itself has much effect on graduates' salaries or career attainment." The most interesting point, from our perspective, that the authors make is that, "a large body of evidence suggests that the curriculum taught in business schools has only a small relationship to what is important for succeeding in business."

By far the most widely used argument against fully participative management is that employees are not knowledgeable enough or that they are not prepared to accept the responsibility. Those that are not prepared to accept the responsibility will not succeed and are increasingly being weeded out and replaced by those that are willing to. As for those that lack the knowledge, Thomas Jefferson provided the answer most eloquently on September 28, 1820:

> **"I know of no safe depository of the ultimate powers**
> **of the society but the people themselves,**
> **and if we think them not enlightened enough to**
> **exercise their control with a wholesome discretion,**
> **the remedy is not to take it from them,**
> **but to inform their discretion."**

Chapter IV

START RIGHT; HIRE RIGHT!

"If you had hired the right person in the first place *# *!!,
we wouldn't . . . ."

—Anonymous (but frequent)

Avoid significant grief! Get it right in the first place!

Most organizations and their managers spend far too little time
on the whole process of recruitment, selection, and interviewing.
Employees are seen primarily as *resources* that can easily be purchased
and discarded as required. The whole process is frequently viewed
as a boring waste of time, sitting there having to interview several
candidates and asking the same types of questions over and over
again. It is considered a chore that can be farmed out to the Human
Resource Department or, worse yet, to an outside agency.

These same organizations will spend thousands of dollars trying to
create a more productive workplace, yet they won't take adequate time to
try and ensure that they have the right employees in the first place; those
who are capable and willing to exhibit the required competencies and
behaviors that constitute a productive workplace culture. Recruitment,
selection, and interviewing is certainly a very tiring process. It is very
difficult to sit and interview four or five candidates for the same position
and to actively listen all day. But if management's primary responsibility

is to create and sustain a productive workplace, then it is a major part of that overall responsibility to hire the right employees in the first place.

Manage your primary risk.

We talk about risk management in every area but staffing. We talk about managing risk in finance, in safety, in quality control, and in production; yet we fail to remember that all of these areas are managed and run by employees. So why not manage your primary risk, which is the quality of your employees? Many organizations, however, rely on policies, rules, regulations, and elaborate processes and procedures to preclude any use of human discretion and minimize the risk of human error. Policies, however, cannot by themselves prevent risk or the necessity for human discretion. Employees who are knowledgeable, good problem solvers, and able to use their common sense, can do far more for risk management than any number of policies. So why not hire employees who exhibit and possess such competencies and behaviors in the first place? Jeffrey Pfeffer (1998, p. 64) says that:

"Selective hiring of new personnel is one of the seven practices of successful organizations."

The traditional methods of recruitment have been negative in their approach. What I mean is that we have taken a group of candidates, weeded out those who clearly do not meet the minimum requirements in the areas of knowledge, skills, and experience and then through some process of rating and elimination we are left with one candidate who is selected, in effect, by default. We have not, however, really proven that the selected candidate can do all that we want and require and that he or she truly has the best *fit* for the job. A more positive approach is to clearly determine what overall competencies and behaviors are required and to then prove to everyone's satisfaction which candidate actually possesses those requirements and truly fits both the job and the organizational culture.

Competencies and behaviors

First of all, competencies and behaviors should be defined. The obvious ones that we have traditionally based our hiring on are such things as knowledge, skills, and experience. These are usually quite easily identified from the candidates' résumés. The more important ones, however, are hidden from view and not that easily identified. What traits and behaviors do the applicants normally portray at work? Do they show initiative? Are they good problem solvers? Do they work well in a team environment? Do they put the customer first even under trying circumstances? How do they handle conflict and stress? What is their interpersonal behavior like? The answers to these questions are not found on a résumé. They are crucial, however, to obtaining employees who fit into a productive workplace environment, which was discussed earlier. As one expert puts it, "People are hired for their technical knowledge, promoted for their innovation, and fired for their interpersonal behavior."

Take, for example, the position of a receptionist. You may have an applicant who has 10 years of experience, can keyboard 80 words a minute error free in between calls and visitors, and can fill in for accounts payable at the same time. If she or he cannot, however, talk to callers and greet visitors in a courteous and friendly manner at all times, then the applicant cannot do the job well. But we don't normally test for or determine whether or not the applicant has such competencies and behaviors and they cannot be determined from a résumé.

How do we then determine the competencies and behaviors of an applicant? First we need to fully define and describe what it is that we are looking for. These are referred to as the Selection Criteria. Legally speaking, as long as we are looking for bona fide occupational requirements (BFOR) and bona fide occupational qualifications (BFOQ), we are free to stipulate the competencies and behaviors that are required. In the case of a receptionist, for example, we would stipulate that the successful candidate must have a courteous, friendly, and helpful approach to all callers and visitors, even at times of pressure. We then need to structure the interview in such a manner that we ask questions that are designed to determine whether or not the applicant does actually possess and has demonstrated the use of such competencies and behaviors. For the receptionist applicants we would ask such questions as, "Describe a situation where you have had an irate customer and how you handled them." We are not asking them how they *might* handle such a hypothetical situation. It does not take a genius to understand the response that is expected; if they don't possess that minimum amount of intelligence then they don't deserve any further interview time. What we do ask is how they *have* handled such an actual situation. We are asking for hard proof rather than just "gut feel." This, as discussed later, can be further verified in the reference checking process. This type of questioning is usually referred to as Behavioral Descriptive Interviewing.

You can further validate the required competencies and behaviors, at least in the case of a prospective receptionist, by asking the applicant to do the job on a casual basis for a day or two and allow everyone to observe and assess the applicant's abilities. In other situations, especially managerial ones, it is extremely useful to have the final few applicants spend at least one full day in the department in which they are going to work and in the organization in general. They can ask questions of whomever they want and be asked questions by the employees in return. In this manner the organization can obtain valuable feedback from both the employees and other managers and can also ask the applicants what impressions they gained and what ideas they might have as a result in order to better assess the applicants' abilities and potential *fit*. You might also ask the applicants to assess the particular work area and provide a quick report as to how well they feel the organization is performing and what they would do to improve it.

It is always advisable to have more than one individual involved in the entire recruitment process; different people notice different things about each applicant and it provides a far greater degree of objectivity. By all means listen to your "gut feel", that little inner voice of experience that's trying to tell you something, but it should be tempered by the judgement of others. A small panel of people that represent different aspects of the organization that are relevant to the position being applied for is desirable. In the case of the receptionist you would, of course, have the direct supervisor involved, but you might also include another manager and a peer or, if possible, the incumbent who is leaving. If an applicant is applying for a position that is part of a team, you might consider having the team do the selection. Peer input is usually far more insightful than that of the supervisor; they understand the job demands far better and they are in the best position to determine true organizational and team fit.

Always check references.

The next critical step, which is frequently not done or not done very thoroughly, is to check references. Written references, for the most part, are not worth the paper that they are written on. I have frequently had to write "references" for people who were terminated for poor performance as part of their settlement package. It is amazing how much can be said without saying anything significant. What is required are verbal references so that there is ample opportunity in conversation to probe, clarify, and follow through on different pieces of information that might come to light. These references should be from sources that you can trust to provide you with honest and open feedback regarding the applicant's work and not from his or her friends, physician, or parish priest.

Easier said than done you might very well say. Some organizations, as a matter of policy, do not provide references; this is usually a reaction to any potential legal threat. Most give vague, broad-brush answers that tell you very little. Human Resource Departments are very skilled at answering your questions, but divulging nothing of consequence. Despite these potential difficulties, you can usually obtain valuable feedback if you persist; and you should persist. Do you buy a car without fully checking out its performance and maintenance record as well as the warrantee? Do you buy purely on "gut feel"? Then why do the same when hiring an employee that is probably going to cost you far more than a car?

Referees should be those that can answer questions about the applicant's past and or present business experience. They should always include the applicant's current supervisor. If applicants are concerned about their current employer becoming aware of their looking elsewhere, then the reference can be made contingent upon them otherwise being the successful applicant. If applicants are concerned, because they do not get along well with their current supervisor or because they were terminated for some reason, they should still be able to provide their supervisor as a referee and to explain the circumstances. Personality clashes do occur. People also get terminated for many reasons other than poor performance. They may not have *fit* their past employer, but may still be a perfect candidate for your organization. How they explain the circumstances should also provide you with more valuable insight into the *true* applicant.

The questions asked of referees should, wherever possible, refer back to the behavioral descriptive questions that were asked in the job interview. Remember that these questions are designed to obtain factual examples of past work that illustrate the competencies and behaviors of the applicant. So when talking with referees, they should be asked to validate the specific examples provided by the applicant wherever possible. If the applicant, for example, said that he or she designed a completely new work procedure on their own that saved the company thousands of dollars, then ask his or her past supervisor whether or not this was the case. It may have been, but it may also have been true that the applicant designed this new procedure with the help of several other team members. Asking such specific questions is also a great help in getting referees to talk as they have something specific to answer rather than a vague question, for example, dealing with the applicant's strengths or weaknesses.

One last question that should usually be asked is, "Would you rehire this person?" This puts the referee squarely on the spot. As mentioned above, some organizations do not provide any references because they are concerned about possible legal ramifications. They are entitled to do that. It should be noted, however, that an employer, if they do give a reference, is legally obliged to give an honest one or face being sued by the subsequent employer of the applicant in question.

The best references are usually the informal ones.

How can one check references unless the applicant formally provides them? This is still a free country and nothing prevents one from networking and asking someone else's opinion of the applicant. You may not wish to let them know that the applicant has applied for a position with your organization, but you can still find ways of eliciting useful information. If the applicant asks you not to contact their current employer, then don't. But you may very well know someone who belongs to the same professional association or someone who does business with the applicant on a regular basis. These are by far the best references that you can get because they are freely given by people whom you know and respect in the same area of work. Use your networks to the utmost.

There is all too often the idea or feeling that checking references or asking specific and demanding questions in an interview is an intrusion into a person's private affairs. This is probably partly due to the "rights" culture that has become part of our society. And no doubt that it is an intrusion; one that should be diligently pursued at all costs for the benefit of the organization as a whole and the benefit of all future coworkers. If you apply for a job, you should expect to be thoroughly grilled. This is also to the applicant's benefit. The more thorough the recruitment process, the better chance that those selected will fit the organization and be successful.

Some organizations like to rely on various psychological tests to determine and verify an applicant's general competencies and behaviors. If recruiting for the police force, it is understandable that one would want to try and determine the applicant's overall psychological makeup. For most other types of general jobs in society, however, it is far more practical and accurate to determine the applicant's proven track record through behavioral descriptive interviewing and thorough reference checking. I would far rather rely on an applicant's proven track record for determining initiative and teamwork, for example, than the results of some psychological test. I recall early on in my career being tested for a sales position. One of the multiple choice questions asked whether or not I preferred staying home with my stamp collection, reading a book, or going out with the boys for a beer on Friday night. Guess which answer was the desired one?

The applicant's track record may be further substantiated or refuted through such practical tests as letting him or her actually try the position, as with the example of the receptionist above. In the case of specific skills such as keyboarding ability, mathematical calculations, and spatial awareness, for example, it is always a valid process to test the applicant if there is any doubt as to ability or competence.

In summary, if you wish to avoid significant grief, then spend the time up front in hiring the right staff. The cost of poor hiring can be enormous. Consider the potential costs of advertising, time spent in the recruitment process, training, performance management, overtime to cover the vacant position, poor morale of coworkers, lost productivity, and possible legal fees and severance pay.

Remember if management's primary responsibility is to create and sustain a productive workplace, then it is a major part of that overall responsibility to hire the right staff in the first place.

> **Recruitment, selection, and interviewing is a very time consuming process when done well; it should be.**

Chapter V

STAFF DEVELOPMENT

"Companies that don't encourage employee education
of all kinds are dumb."

—Tom Peters

Productive workplaces, without exception, place a great deal of emphasis on staff training and development because they recognize that the performance of their employees represents the only sustainable competitive advantage that they possibly might have over other organizations. These organizations spend time and money, even in tough economic times, to develop employees on an on-going basis in order to nurture and sustain the advantage they can provide. In this manner they are able to ensure that all employees understand and follow the core principles of a productive workplace and avoid the costly "flavor of the month" syndrome.

There is another pressing reason today for developing employees. Qualified people are in short supply in many fields of work and the aging population only exacerbates this problem. Most employers don't have the money to compete with the very large industries. Even if they did, they can't *buy* employees for any length of time before someone outbids them. You can't wait for our educational institutions to catch up; there's always a cyclical time lag between the supply of graduates and the demand for them. Besides you need well-experienced and qualified people in many positions, not recent graduates without any experience.

Internship programs are great, but suffer from the same problem as they are normally geared only to recent graduates.

**There's really only one viable alternative:
train your valued staff and keep training at all times.**

Qualified employees are needed now, not five or ten years from now after they have gained the required experience and hands-on knowledge. It only makes good business sense to train your own existing staff so that you're better prepared at all times for the loss of staff, organizational growth, and cyclical demands. You will also gain a more productive, creative and innovative workforce.

Jobs vs Work

Unfortunately most organizations suffer from adherence to a very traditional mind-set that views work in terms of discrete jobs that are filled by recruiting people who have already acquired the specific education, training, and experience required for the job. As pointed out by William Bridges (1994) in *Job Shift*, however, this approach can get in the way of the work that needs to be done, because we learn to focus narrowly on the *job* rather than the overall work. Rigid job descriptions are one of the organizational inhibitors to a productive workplace; they constrain delegation of responsibility and lead to the "It's not in my job description" mentality.

What is desperately needed is a new outlook that views the workforce in a more fluid and less rigid and compartmentalized manner. All employees need to be valued, not only for their specific skills, but also for their overall intrinsic ability and desire to learn and problem solve, so that their talents can be applied to the work in general throughout the organization. This is part of the required shift in management thinking that has been so well articulated by Peter Senge (1990) in *The Fifth Discipline: The Art and Practice of the Learning Organization*.

Types of staff development

Staff development is by no means purely a question of providing training in specific skills such as word processing, operating machinery, or doing accounts payable. These types of technical skills are usually taken for granted; either you have them or you don't get the job. Staff development also involves other important areas such as:

- **Training current or future managers in effective management practices** that foster and sustain a productive workplace. One poor manager, who fails to provide proper leadership, has a far greater negative impact on overall productivity, service, and quality than one poorly qualified subordinate. A manager's people and leadership skills are of far more importance than technical know-how, as we shall see in Chapter XIV.
- **Ensuring that all employees share the same organizational vision, mission and values**. All staff must march to the same tune and need to be constantly reminded as to what the organizational goals are and what principles they must adhere to. This is especially critical in today's participative workplace, where employees are expected to make independent decisions in the interests of good customer service.
- **Sharing organizational performance information with all employees on an on-going basis** so that everyone is able to make informed decisions and have input. The greater the information that is shared, the more able employees are to make decisions that are in the organization's best interests.
- **Providing performance feedback to all employees on a regular and on-going basis** to assist them in their development and career planning. We all need feedback, not only to do our work well and to learn, but also to feel that someone really does care and appreciates our efforts; a simple "thank you" is one of the most effective motivators ever devised.
- **Ensuring that all employees are as multi-skilled and cross-trained as possible** so that there is maximum flexibility and cost effectiveness in staff coverage and manpower planning. You are not caught short because someone is off sick, on

37

vacation, or decides to retire. You are not caught short when you need someone to work overtime or because of sudden changes in production requirements. Employees also benefit from obtaining additional skills, abilities, and knowledge and from having less restrictive and less boring work.

- **Establishing more apprenticeship programs**, not just the formal existing programs in most trades, but internal ones that are specific to the unique demands of the individual organization. We need to plan our manpower needs and create our own apprenticeship programs to meet them. This also makes it far easier to attract and retain staff if they know that they are going to benefit from the training provided and have some career growth, rather than just be hired into a specific pigeonhole with a hit or miss chance of advancing. Some manufacturers have significantly reduced their turnover by adopting such a philosophy.

- **Providing work specific training**, as there are positions that by their very nature do not have any specific educational or training program. The position of public works superintendent, for example, requires a good general background in a number of different areas. Well qualified people in this field have usually acquired their expertise by working in a variety of positions and taking a broad variety of training on their own initiative in such areas as water and waste water treatment, road maintenance, facilities maintenance, preventative maintenance, capital planning, and many other areas of technical and managerial expertise. Because of the lack of training, qualified individuals are extremely scarce in this area.

- **Ensuring that there is appropriate succession planning.** Many organizations are having difficulty in filling key positions, because no thought was ever given to developing a successor to the incumbent who was retiring. It is far more cost effective, organizationally more efficient, and better for staff morale to train successors internally.

- **Ensuring that all employees have the required competencies and behaviors.** These are not taught for the most part in any formal educational program, yet they are critical for employees to be able to fulfill their responsibilities in the most effective manner. A receptionist with a poor telephone manner or the inability to deal with an irate customer, for example, is not performing effectively no matter how skilled he or she is at word processing or handling customer accounts. One representative of the hospitality industry says that they "hire the ones who smile and teach them the rest." It is said that most people are terminated for the lack of interpersonal skills that are required by their position, not because of a lack of technical expertise.

- **Assisting Boards, Councils and work teams to be more effective** by providing such training as Effective Meeting Skills, Problem Solving, and Conflict Resolution. Boards of Directors, elected Councils and general work teams need the skills that allow them to work together effectively as a group and to effectively utilize and manage their diverse skills, knowledge, and personalities.

Employers cannot and should not depend on educational institutions and government programs to provide employees with those skills that meet their unique organizational requirements; they should be constantly training their own employees to meet their own needs, both current and future.

Many organizations are exacerbating an already difficult labor market by replacing older more experienced and more knowledgeable employees with younger ones who are less costly. This practice is extremely shortsighted and only harms the organization's ability to compete. These same organizations frequently wind up hiring many of these skilled workers back on contract, because they cannot replace the knowledge and experience.

What is needed is greater flexibility in retaining older employees on some sort of a part-time basis so that their knowledge is not lost and so that they can impart this knowledge to younger employees in both a formal manner and as a mentor where appropriate.

Not only is too little time and money spent on staff development at the best of times, but this is all too often cut back or eliminated when times get tough. This is a very short sighted and counter productive practice. When times get tough you need all the motivation, input, and productivity that you can get from all of your staff. Today's employees also wish to work in a productive workplace and they demand appropriate training.

Staff development is a necessity, not a luxury.

Chapter VI

MANAGING PERFORMANCE

If, as said earlier, management's primary responsibility is to ensure a productive workplace where employees at all levels are fully motivated, then certainly performance management is one of management's main functions; yet it is also the most neglected. Poor performance management, or the avoidance of it, is the most frequently encountered organizational problem in our consulting experience and is also the root cause of so many others that may not initially be diagnosed as such.

What is performance management?

The term "performance management" means the overall direction and support of employee performance from the time that they first start to the time that they leave. The process begins with effective orientation to the organization and to the job. It includes staff development, coaching, *self* and *other* assessment tools, career coaching and planning, counseling, and ongoing formal and informal feedback from a variety of sources including internal and external customers. Yes it does also include discipline, but only to be used as a last resort except in the case of overtly poor performance. Discipline is not something to be used to correct legitimate mistakes or typical behavior; it doesn't work and the problems remain.

Traditional performance evaluation

Most organizations, however, still rely on the traditional concept and practice of performance evaluation as opposed to performance management. Performance evaluation, in and of itself, however, is a useless and unfair practice. Traditionally, performance evaluation has been used to:

- Provide the employee with feedback regarding overall performance and to rate the performance.
- Identify strengths, weaknesses and plans for improvement.
- Document which goals have been achieved and which have not.
- Improve individual performance and organizational productivity.
- Document acceptable evidence of poor performance for successful dismissal for cause.

None of these points, however, can be successfully achieved through periodic performance evaluation. Providing performance feedback regarding both strengths and weaknesses on an annual, or even semi-annual basis is meaningless; feedback, both positive and negative, must be immediate in order to have any relevance and to be effective.

Performance must be managed as and when required.

Letting performance problems remain unattended until the next evaluation is counterproductive; they must be dealt with immediately or else the behavior is, in effect, condoned. If nothing is said or done at the actual time, the presumption is that the performance problem wasn't deemed to be serious enough to warrant any action. In cases of wrongful dismissal, the courts will invariably see it this way as well. They will also say that no attempt was made at the time of the behavior to rectify it and that there was no pattern of progressive discipline. Specific constructive criticism or discipline must occur at the time of the actual problem.

Saving all feedback for the time of the evaluation makes the process disciplinary in nature rather than supportive and does nothing, therefore, to foster and sustain better performance and productivity.

Blanchard and Johnson (1983, p.83) refer to it as the "Leave them alone and then ZAP" syndrome.

Productive review of performance

If you must have some form of formal assessment and documentation of performance, then let it be purely a *review* of past performance. A productive review of performance that is part of ongoing performance management provides a formal opportunity to mutually review individual performance in its entire context. Such a review should allow both parties to:

- Discuss and agree on what organizational and performance goals have been accomplished, what are the future goals, and what the priorities are.
- Discuss and agree on what training, including competencies and behaviors, would be beneficial to the employee and the organization.
- Discuss and agree on what organizational and managerial changes would facilitate better employee performance.
- Obtain and discuss feedback from other interested parties such as subordinates, peers, and internal and external customers. Peter Block (1993, p.153) says, "If you insist on having an appraisal process, let people be appraised by their customers."
- Discuss and plan career options.

As mentioned above, there are no surprises in this process; all performance "issues" have already been addressed as and when required. The review, therefore, is not a disciplinary process; it is an opportunity for both parties to discuss all aspects of performance and to agree on what is mutually beneficial to both the organization and the employee.

Again let me reiterate that a performance review, even if done in the most supportive and productive manner, is no substitute at all for ongoing performance management. The former is purely an opportunity for formal discussion and documentation, whereas the latter is what truly matters in shaping an employee's performance and behavior.

Performance management is supportive, but firm.

Performance management does not mean a top-down, heavy-handed approach. What it does mean is a supportive but firm approach and the creation of an ongoing learning environment where employees welcome helpful feedback and the opportunity to learn, improve, and gain the overall competencies that will enhance their performance and their careers.

It is the disciplinary aspect, however, that most of us immediately think of when we talk about managing performance. This, in itself, is indicative of how neglected this whole area of managing employee performance is. We only think of the rather narrow and punitive aspect of this critically important function. Because the positive aspects of coaching and training, for example, are neglected, performance issues magnify to the point that all patience is lost and it is only discipline that is viewed as a cure. Ironically, however, the whole issue of discipline including termination, as we shall see in the following chapter, is also neglected and most often avoided.

First of all, proper orientation of all employees to both the organization and their job can prevent any number of issues. Employees should be given a very clear understanding of what the expectations are for both their technical performance and their behavior. They should be given a clear understanding of what the organizational values are and how they are expected to behave with each other and with customers, for example. This, in our experience, is rarely done. It is assumed that employees will pick these things up on their own accord and learn to fit in.

If the appropriate knowledge, skill, or behavior is shown to be lacking, then immediate assistance in the form of training and coaching should be offered. Most managers think nothing of coaching their own children or the local Minor League ball team, yet they seldom think to apply the same principles to the staff that they work with. The principles and steps of effective coaching are quite simple and well known:

- Describe the behavior that needs changing and the ramifications to the employee and the organization of that behavior. Provide specific examples; do not generalize.

- Identify, describe and demonstrate the alternative appropriate behavior.
- Observe the employee's attempts to model the alternative behavior and continue to describe and demonstrate the required behavior until the employee has succeeded.
- Be supportive at all times.

As stated earlier, this is not a disciplinary process. There is a critically important distinction, put forward by Blanchard and Johnson (1983), that must be made here:

If they don't know, coach.
If they do know, reprimand.

When trying to address problems of personal behavior, which admittedly are difficult to deal with, the use of self assessment and feedback tools may be of great assistance in helping employees become aware of their damaging behavior, so that they can begin to address it and so that any attempt at coaching will not be rejected. Receiving feedback from your boss is one thing, whereas receiving it from your peers, subordinates and customers has an entirely different impact. That is why assessment and feedback tools that obtain feedback both from the employee concerned and from others in the work place are so powerful.

Avoiding performance issues

The avoidance of dealing with performance issues is, as previously stated, the biggest organizational problem that my partners and I encounter. The problem is so prevalent that there are countless examples of such creative attempts at avoidance.

Teambuilding workshops are frequently an avoidance of dealing with individual performance issues. Good teamwork is an example of a competency that most organizations demand of their employees today. Organizations frequently express interest in teambuilding and building greater teamwork and cooperation within the organization. The reasons for any lack of teamwork and cooperation, however, are frequently the result of individual performance issues that have not been addressed. This is frequently passed off by saying that the group just can't get along because of the personalities involved or because so-and-so has a strong overriding personality or because someone else is too much of a prima donna. The list of possible reasons is endless, but little is done to resolve the actual issues with the individuals concerned. This is avoided and a blanket approach is used with all employees in the group under the guise of teambuilding.

This approach does not and cannot work. It is purely a strategy of avoidance that annoys everyone in the group. The rest of the group knows fully well which employees do not contribute to their overall teamwork and they resent being categorized in the same manner. The employees responsible for the poor teamwork, on the other hand, still do not understand that their behavior has to change and that others are forced to find ways of working around it. They are let off the hook, so to speak, by acting as if it is a group problem. Some of these issues could have at best been avoided or at least alleviated by explaining thoroughly upon orientation that teamwork and good cooperation is expected. This may have to be followed up with appropriate coaching, but at least the door has been opened because the behavioral expectations have already been clearly spelled out.

Another prevalent issue is poor managerial or supervisory style. How much turnover and loss of good competent employees is due to poor management or supervision? Perhaps an autocratic, gruff management style was the norm a generation ago. But times have changed and so have the expectations of today's workforce. They don't expect to be sworn at or chastised for every little mistake, especially when they are new on the job and learning. Needless to say, this type of management style has always been counterproductive.

Today, however, it is just not tolerated and employees can and will leave and work elsewhere. Yet many organizations are still reluctant to deal with such behavior. They say, "Oh well, that's just Harry, and we all know what he's like." The organization does not explain up front what behavior is not acceptable and then they don't offer any help or assistance in changing that behavior and wonder why they have such high turnover in that supervisor's area.

Withholding pay increases is another prevalent means of avoiding performance problems. Many organizations have compensation plans that have provision for annual increases based on merit or performance. If performance is lacking, the increase may be withheld or only partially granted. This does nothing, however, to improve performance; it is purely a disciplinary measure. This issue will be discussed further in a later chapter on rewards.

The use of various programs and consultants in Conflict Resolution, Relationship Building, Commitment to Organizational and Behavioral Principles, Facilitation and Mediation, are also, in many instances, purely examples of avoiding what are usually well known and acknowledged individual performance issues that no one is willing to address. As stated above, this blanket approach does not work; the rest of the group knows fully well which employees are causing the problems and they resent being categorized in the same manner. They view such attempts at problem resolution as a farce and readily see that their management does not have the backbone to really come to grips with the actual problems. This is demoralizing.

Employee appreciation plans such as free pizza for lunch, tickets to the ball game, and other similar plans are also frequently used to mask and calm serious performance issues that are a disruption to the work area in question. Such plans, under these circumstances, have the reverse effect; they are not perceived as appreciation and are ridiculed as being symptomatic of management's inability to manage properly

Forcing an employee to quit by picking on them is also a frequently used means of avoiding properly dealing with a performance problem. Give the employee all the undesirable jobs and unwanted shifts. This is a cowardly means of avoiding telling the employee precisely what the problems are and what the expected behaviors are to rectify them.

Why performance issues must be addressed.

Many organizations, from our experience, do not see the importance of dealing with such issues. The product is still being manufactured, the service is being provided, the organization is functioning, and the company is profitable, so why should they be concerned? Production, quality, and service, however, could all be improved and, if they don't perform to their utmost ability, they will be less able to deal with future growth, economic downturns, increased competition, and less available resources. The most crucial problem that they will face, however, is the inability to attract and retain competent talent. Talented people today can afford to be choosy and they are. They research the organizations that they would like to work for, where they feel that their talents will be nurtured, and where they will have an opportunity to grow and learn. They resent having to work in an environment where one doesn't have the opportunity to learn and benefit from the experience of other competent people, because of a lack of ongoing performance management.

A productive workplace requires ongoing performance management.

Chapter VII

PRODUCTIVE TERMINATION

"One bad apple can spoil the whole barrel."

—Old proverb.

This book is solely about building productive workplaces that foster and promote employees' intrinsic motivation and responsibility through a fully participative management style and related management practices. It may seem strange, or out of place, therefore, to devote an entire chapter to the subject of termination as it has such a negative and authoritarian connotation. The reality, however, is that workplaces cannot be productive unless one is prepared to terminate employees when all else fails. As much as one may take the positive view that all employees come to work prepared to do a good job, the fact remains that some employees do not fit and some, for whatever reason, do not wish to fit. It is critical to the success of a productive workplace that such employees be terminated. The old proverb that "one bad apple can spoil the whole barrel" is all too true.

Termination can and should be productive for all concerned.

The earlier it is done, the more productive it can be. Not to terminate someone for justifiable reasons such as poor performance, lack of fit, or plain position redundancy is misguided compassion at best. At worst, which is usually the norm, it is a flagrant abdication of management responsibility, which may cause severe harm to both the organization and the person concerned.

Excuses for avoiding the issue

How often have you heard or used these excuses for not dealing with issues that clearly warrant termination:

- We're trying to be compassionate.
- We don't wish to damage the employee's career and reputation.
- We're waiting for the next performance evaluation.
- We don't wish to upset all the other staff.
- It will reflect on our own hiring and judgement.
- It will be too disruptive and costly.
- The situation will improve with time.

The list is endless and excuses are especially prevalent for higher-level positions where, ironically, the greatest damage may be done to both the individual and the organization. We severely delude ourselves with these excuses. Ignoring poor performance, lack of fit, or position redundancy is neither compassionate nor understanding and does nothing to help the individuals concerned, other staff, the organization as a whole, the manager, or board/council responsible.

The employees concerned are harmed.

Ignoring the problem wastes whatever talents they do have and delays the acquisition of required training, competencies, and behaviors. They lack the required motivation to learn what is required for their own personal success. They also find themselves stuck in a job that they are not suited for and where their incompetence only generates disrespect. The longer the delay in dealing with the problem, the worse it becomes and the more likely that there will be an abrupt and adversarial severance that does nothing to help them understand or come to grips with the issues.

Ignoring the problem severely affects other staff.

As subordinates they lack appropriate direction, coaching, performance management, and recognition. They also have to constantly cover for the boss or share in the disrespect for that particular department or work area. As peers they have to pick up the slack as well as watch someone frequently receive the same rewards for incompetent or unnecessary work; there is no incentive for excellence and productivity.

The organization as a whole suffers.

The organization suffers from lost productivity, poor morale, poor service, and a general lack of incentive and acceptance of responsibility; the higher the level of the position the greater the negative impact. The manager or board/council responsible suffers because they will eventually be held accountable; and the longer the delay, the greater the amount of any severance package that will ultimately have to be paid.

Abdication of the responsibility to deal with such issues is unfair and irresponsible to the individual concerned and the organization as a whole. All too often the end result is a termination that takes place in an adversarial and acrimonious manner that is of no benefit to either party. This responsibility is also frequently abdicated to organizational consultants who are contracted to resolve organizational issues without being told that there are underlying performance issues, which are well known to the organization, but which have never been addressed. When the issues are then finally confronted and the employee terminated, there is the hypocrisy of those who were aware of the problems, who complained about the problems, who did nothing about the problems, and yet express concern, sorrow and even anger over the termination. Consultants, unfortunately, experience this situation time and time again.

The earlier the better.

Such issues must be dealt with as soon as they arise for the benefit of all concerned. They must be dealt with immediately through ongoing performance management, rather than waiting for some annual, ineffective, and usually neglected, appraisal process. The greater the delay, the more chance there is that the performance problem is, in effect, condoned and the less the chance for any effective remedial action. The greater the delay, the more chance there is that the employee has lost too much respect to remain in the organization. The greater the delay, the more chance there is of being boxed in by the legal ramifications of constructive and wrongful dismissal. The sooner that the issues are dealt with, the greater the opportunity for other options that can benefit both the employee and the organization:

- Coaching in the required skills, competencies and behaviors.
- Finding another more suitable position without great loss of face.
- Amicably agreeing that the employee should look for another job.
- Helping the employee understand that he or she should resign.
- Helping the employee with appropriate career coaching.

These options are only available through ongoing performance management and early intervention. None of these options, however, may be successful. The lack of fit may be so great that no amount of coaching will succeed and there is no other option than termination. At an early stage, however, termination is far less damaging to the employee as he or she can always say that they quickly realized that this was the wrong job for them and can get on with their career without the loss of respect. The legal issues and potential cost at such an early stage are also far less.

So many organizations today are seeking to create a more participative and productive workplace. What they all too often forget, however, is that such a workplace needs constant care and attention to ensure that all employees fit the desired organizational culture.

This requires ongoing performance management that, in turn, may require termination—the earlier the better.

Chapter VIII

ORGANIZATIONAL STRUCTURE
FLATTER IS BETTER

"Hierarchy is an organization with its face toward the CEO and its ass toward the customer. Pleasing the boss should never be more important than pleasing the customer."

—John F. Welch, Jr.
Chairman and CEO, General Electric, 1981-2001

Increase in organizational democracy

The traditional management style was to control the way people work; to control what they do, how they do it, and virtually every other aspect of their work. This was referred to as Scientific Management and was the primary function of the manager. Most successful organizations today, however, understand that a more democratic and participative management style is more productive and that the traditional style is no longer accepted by most employees, especially a better educated and younger workforce. The increased use of Information Technology has also made organizational communication and reporting so much easier, so that old-fashioned control is no longer required for accountability and reporting requirements.

For many years now we have been talking instead about participative management, self managed teams, delegated responsibility and authority, empowerment, and the rise of organizational democracy in general. The traditional management position that did most of the controlling is being removed from many organizations. As stated earlier, "No one should be able to make a living simply planning, watching, controlling, or evaluating the actions of others." (Block, 1993, p.66)

Managers, of course, are still here today, but their role has significantly changed and sometimes their title. They are expected to be coaches, mentors, trainers, and facilitators who support rather than control and who are just as likely to be called team leader as manager or supervisor.

The Redundancy Hierarchy Test

The title of the position, be it supervisor, manager, director, or vice president is not the critical issue here. I use the term management and manager here in the generic sense. What is the issue is whether a management position is purely one of control or whether it has a legitimate role. Michael Goold and Andrew Campbell (2002, p.278) in *Designing Effective Organizations* propose nine tests for effective organizational design. The "Redundancy Hierarchy Test" poses the question, "Are all levels in the hierarchy and all responsibilities retained by higher levels based on a knowledge and competence advantage?" They write that the purpose of the test is to ensure that the higher levels in an organizational hierarchy have clear value adding roles and that they must be built around a logic that explains why that higher level is better able to contribute than the lower level. They point out that there are inevitable costs to any extra layer of hierarchy and that those costs should be more than offset by an increase in the productivity of the programs beneath them. In the public sector, any redundant layer of hierarchy detracts from scarce funds that could be more productively spent elsewhere and also represents an unnecessary cost to the taxpayer.

Why keep the traditional hierarchical organizational structure?

If it is generally recognized and accepted that the traditional management style is no longer productive, then why do so many cling to the traditional hierarchical organizational structure? Why do three or four or five program managers, for example, automatically require a director to *oversee* them or to *coordinate* their programs? Are they not competent enough to be responsible for their programs? Are they not capable of collaborating and cooperating with each other as required? A major public sector employer, for example, was recently searching for a general manager to oversee the departments of Finance, Human Resources, Information Technology, and Legal Services. What on earth needs overseeing? What needs coordinating, especially among such disparate functions? Presumably each area has a competent and well-trained manager who should be responsible and accountable for his or her own department, including the required teamwork with all other departments.

Another, by no means unique, example is a municipal Community Services Department where the director has to oversee the programs of Recreation, Family and Community Support Services, Bylaw Enforcement, and the Fire department. Each program has its own manager. There is no common functionality or linkage, so what needs to be coordinated? Of course all the programs offer community services, but so does the entire municipality. What actually does the director have as discrete responsibilities? What does the director bring to the table that the program managers do not or cannot? In many cases the answer is nothing. The position has been created purely to group together certain programs because of the traditional mind-set that says that they have to be controlled and that the management span of control is limited and, therefore, one cannot have too many managers reporting directly to the chief administrative officer (CAO) in this example or a chief executive officer (CEO) in the private sector.

But that's exactly the point—there's that word "control" again. If we accept that this traditional management style is dead, or should be, then why are we still using traditional organizational concepts that support it? If we accept a different management style and overall organizational culture, then the question of traditional "span of control" no longer applies. Rather than span of control, a new term such as "span of reporting relationships" would be more appropriate. Certainly there is a limit to how many positions can effectively report to one CAO or CEO, but that limit is far greater than the usual three to five under a traditional control oriented management style. If responsibility is truly delegated to competent managers, it is not at all difficult to have far more direct reports. If the Fire Department, in the above municipal example, reports directly to the CAO, how often does the CAO really need to meet with the fire chief? How much time really needs to be spent directing the fire chief? Can the CAO really provide any direction assuming that he or she lacks the required knowledge and competence? So any reporting is probably only in emergencies or over budgetary issues or broad issues of strategic planning. As the same criteria can be applied to all other functions, the span of direct reports to the CAO can be much broader than ever before. There are also significant advantages to the CAO or CEO to have a broader management team as discussed below.

In the example above of a municipal Community Services Department, the position of director is redundant, as it has no added value; it contributes nothing more than the individual program managers do. On the other hand, take the example of a Community and Economic Development department that included such programs as Recreation, Family and Community Support Services, Tourism, Community Events, and Economic Development. In this case we have a department that is comprised of programs that have strong linkages, and if the director has the functional knowledge and competence in the main area of community/economic development, then he or she can truly add value not only through his or her own functional expertise, but also by uniting and coordinating all programs and resources towards the same goals.

Traditional organizational structure and management style

The traditional hierarchical organizational structure and the traditional management style were mutually supportive and dependent upon each other. Traditional managers relied on power and status to exercise control. The traditional organizational hierarchy was based on levels of power and status and provided for such positions of control, whereas there is no room for such positions in a flat organizational structure.

The hierarchical organizational structure not only supports the concept of management control and the positions that exercise that control, it actually impedes any serious attempt to adopt a more participative and democratic workplace culture:

- The hierarchical structure, by its very nature, forces vertical communication and discourages horizontal communication. It fosters and supports individual silos that do not have to communicate and cooperate with each other.
- The hierarchy of control stands squarely in the way of delegated responsibility and, therefore, breeds irresponsibility and a lack of accountability. One can always pass the buck up the chain of command rather than be accountable.
- Teamwork in general, and cross-functional teams in particular, requires freedom of horizontal communication, which is impeded by a vertical structure.
- Participative management cannot exist in the traditional hierarchy; the two are mutually exclusive. The hierarchy is based on authority and control as opposed to delegation and participation. You either scrap the hierarchy or give up any pretense of a participative management style.
- A hierarchical structure also reinforces arbitrary differences in the level of rewards, differences that are not based on skill and ability or the level of contribution to the organization and its bottom line. Rewards need not be equal; the marketplace dictates different rewards for different occupations. But other distinctions in level of pay should be based on contribution to the organization, not arbitrary distinctions in power and status.

Flatter is better

In the same manner that the traditional hierarchical organizational structure supports the traditional management style, a flat structure supports, fosters, and reinforces a more participative and productive management style and workplace culture. It will, by its very nature, serve to force such changes.

- The communication is more open, direct, and accurate.
- Individual program managers cannot hide and pass the buck; there is no one to pass it to.
- Managers are forced to work with each other across the organization and not just within the narrow confines of some individual silo.
- The management team is a truly representative team of all programs and not just a few select individuals who presume to speak for others in areas that they have little if any experience with.
- Because the management team is now truly representative of all interests, there is far greater opportunity for open and honest input and dialogue from all areas, and less opportunity for the protection of vested interests or personal power and status. The CAO or CEO can be far better assured, as well as the Council or Board, that all sides to any issue are clearly and openly heard.

Competent chief executive officers and chief administrative officers don't need several vice presidents or general managers or directors to oversee, control, and coordinate competent program heads. Keep it simple, keep it flat, and reap the benefits of a more productive organization.

**Changing the organizational structure
is arguably the most important step in changing the
organizational culture to a more participative one; yet
it is frequently overlooked. Unfortunately, however,
you can't do one without the other. The traditional
management style is dead. Bury the traditional
organizational structure with it.**

Chapter IX

CONTROL—WHO'S IN CHARGE?

"All corporations dream about . . . initiative, but seldom
get it. The reason: Too many controls and too much
supervision stifle the people on the scene. They feel
restricted, intimidated or bored."

—Wayne Calloway, CEO, PepsiCo., 1986-1996

With all this talk about participative management, delegation of
responsibility, relaxing of controls, empowerment of employees, and
democracy in the workplace, many, especially those who are brought up
with the traditional view of management, will ask the question, "Well
that's all well and nice, but who's in charge, who's in control?"

The answer is simple: everyone shares in the overall control of the organization.

This only makes sense, as no one is capable of controlling all aspects
of an organization by themselves or even as a management group.
Sharing the responsibility for control only makes practical sense and is
the best means of risk management.

Most organizations, as discussed earlier, still believe in the traditional
management style where management's role is to control the way people
work; to control what they do, how they do it, and every other aspect of
their work. They may profess a belief in quality management, continuous

improvement, and other productive workplace concepts, but they still use a traditional hierarchical structure top heavy with unnecessary management positions, together with numerous policies, procedures, regulations, rigid and detailed job descriptions, annual performance appraisals, and numerous other means of bureaucratic control. This is the paradox that was discussed earlier on and is the misalignment that sends such contradictory messages to all employees. This misalignment is discussed further in Chapter XI.

Bureaucracy

Bureaucracy is defined by Webster's as, "a system of administration marked by officialism, red tape and proliferation." Most organizations, both public and private, suffer from one degree of bureaucracy or another. Bureaucracy, however, is too slow, too unresponsive, and too incapable of change to survive in this world of rapid ongoing change. Bureaucracy, most importantly, also stands firmly in the way of employee responsibility and accountability at all levels and does little if anything to provide any measure of control over such fundamental issues as quality, service, and safety. No organization, therefore, can operate productively by relying on any great degree of bureaucracy.

Policies

There are two incidents that I always recall when thinking about the usefulness of organizational policies. The first was a presentation to approximately 2000 employees about the introduction of a corporate Quality Management program. As Director of Human Resources, I put an 11 lb., 9 inch thick binder on the podium and asked if anyone knew what it was. No one did. It was the organizational policy manual.

The second was when a client phoned us and wanted to know whether or not they could discipline an employee, as they had no written policy on discipline.

We are so governed by policies, rules, and regulations, especially in the public sector, that in their absence, people stop thinking for themselves and take no action even when required. The process governs instead of the desired result. Policies are all too often misused and undermine the use of practical common sense.

Many organizations rely on policies, rules, regulations, and elaborate processes and procedures to preclude any use of human discretion and to minimize the risk of human error. Policies, however, cannot by themselves prevent risk or the necessity for human discretion. Employees who are knowledgeable and empowered to use their common sense, can do far more for risk management than any number of policies.

> **"The people who know best how the job should be done are the ones doing it."**
>
> **—Dana Corporation,
> One page corporate policy statement.**

Today's organizations require employees who are knowledgeable, well trained, and have the delegated responsibility to make informed decisions that benefit their employer. Good customer service demands that the front line salesperson or receptionist, for example, has the ability and authority to make decisions that require the use of their discretion and common sense. Not all customer questions and needs fit into the neat categories of an automated message center or the predetermined FAQs on a web site. Quality and safety, we are constantly told, is the responsibility of all employees. If that is the case, then even in an assembly line environment, the individual employee must have the delegated responsibility to shut the line down in the event of a perceived emergency or to remove a defective product or component.

Good management practices are good risk management. Good management means delegating responsibility to all employees to make decisions that are based on common sense and the use of a well-informed discretion. If we expect and rely on policies to guide our every action, then we undermine and preclude effective management and create additional risk. Policies are useful tools to provide broad parameters for behavior, but they must be balanced with the use of effective management practices that promote and encourage well informed and responsible employees at all levels in the organization.

Mutual trust and respect and the use of discretion

One of the best examples of the useless attempt at control through rigid policies as opposed to trusting employees and the use of informed discretion is provided by Peter Scholtes (1998, pp.302-303), author of *The Leader's Handbook*. An organization had a typical bereavement leave policy that provided "time off with pay up to a maximum of three (3) working days for working time lost if there is a death in the immediate family . . . . An employee's immediate family will be considered . . . spouse, child, stepchild, mother, father, sister, brother, stepparents, grandparents, and grandchildren of the employee; son-in-law and daughter-in-law; mother, father, sister, brother, and grandparents of the spouse." The policy also stipulated that the leave had to be within a seven-calendar-day period, that one of the days had to be the day of the funeral, that the request must be made to the personnel department and that they may require verification of death and the relationship of the deceased to the employee and other detailed bureaucratic requirements.

The organization changed the policy to one based on trust and respect of the employee: "If you require time off due to the death of a friend or family member, make arrangements with your supervisor."

"What were the results? . . . The total number of days used for bereavement leave under the new policy was 47 percent of days used under the old policy, less than one-half the previous use of bereavement leave."

Rules and Regulations

Ricardo Semler (1993, pp.96-97), CEO of Semco, S.A., has this to say regarding rules and regulations:

> A company makes, sells, bills, and, God willing, collects . . . .
> With few exceptions, rules and regulations only serve to:
>
> - Divert attention away from a company's objectives.
> - Provide a false sense of security for executives.
> - Create work for bean counters.
> - Teach men to stone dinosaurs and start fire with sticks.

The desire for rules and the need for innovation are, I believe, incompatible. Rules freeze companies inside a glacier; innovation lets them ride sleighs over it.

There is another, less obvious dividend to the banishing of rule books: people begin to make more decisions on their own, decisions they are usually better qualified to make than their supervisors.

**"Rule # 1: Use your good judgement in all situations.
There will be no additional rules"**

—Nordstrom Rules

Job Descriptions

We often hear managers talk about the necessity and importance of having clear up-dated job descriptions for all employees. I've made a habit of asking them if they have one themselves; the answer is usually no. I further ask them if they need one to understand what their responsibilities are. They start to look slightly uncomfortable and say no they don't.

So why do all their employees require job descriptions? Are they less intelligent, less responsible, less able to think for themselves? Or do they need to have all of their actions and initiative controlled?

In many unionized environments there is a requirement for detailed job descriptions. This is precisely because so many unions stand in the way of cross-training and multi-skilling as they know that such effective and productive practices may lead to less union membership. Only an electrician is allowed to change a light bulb. The office clerk, who changes them at home all the time, is not allowed to and neither is the carpenter and certainly not the manager who would then be "stealing" union work. This is the mentality that is propagated by the use of your standard detailed job description. This is not a mentality that is conducive to a participative, cost effective workplace, where all employees at all levels need to look at the overall work that has to be accomplished, instead of looking only within the vary narrow confines of their job descriptions.

The traditional job description is outmoded and counter productive in today's workplace. If you want responsible, thinking employees with initiative, then get rid of their detailed job descriptions. Tell your employees what you expect of them, provide them with the appropriate orientation and ongoing training and let them get the work done rather than a narrow list of tasks. The best job description would say only: **"Use Your Common Sense."**

This is a far more successful approach to productivity, quality, safety, and customer service. It is also the best defense for any risk management; employees who can and are allowed to think prevent far more problems than detailed job descriptions and other bureaucratic policies and procedures.

Performance evaluation

Policies and the like are not a substitute for good management. All too often, for example, organizations rely on an elaborate system of performance evaluation yet practice little, if any, ongoing performance management. As pointed out earlier, periodic evaluation is useless without ongoing daily attention to performance in all aspects. This reliance on the formal evaluation lets managers off the hook; they do not then have to provide goals and objectives, to keep employees informed, or coach them when necessary. They avoid daily performance issues and save them for some future magical date when the evaluation is due. This does nothing for effective risk management or even control.

The same manager who insists on such ineffective performance controls, is frequently the same manager who sits behind the desk and has little knowledge of what actually is happening in the workplace on a day-to-day basis. Effective managers spend a great deal of their time out of their offices and practice MBWA or Management By Walking Around. There is no better way of keeping your finger on the pulse of the organization than by roaming around, talking to people, and observing what goes on. If you really want to know what's actually going on in most organizations, you talk to the receptionist, the janitor, or the plant operator. They usually know far more about what's working and what isn't, than the executive sitting in his or her office. This is why it is important to insist on interviewing staff from the bottom up when reviewing an organization's effectiveness.

Customer service

What about customer service? You are going through the cashier with 25 small identical items. You tell the cashier that there are 25 and she nevertheless proceeds to count all of them. What about finding out at the cashier that the item you wish to purchase does not have a bar code on it? You tell the cashier what the price is, but she pages the supervisor. You and the entire line up behind you wait for the supervisor to finally arrive, go to where the item is located to get the price, and then return to the cashier with the information.

Why do these organizations have such policies that prevent any initiative on the part of their front line staff to exercise their discretion to provide good customer service? Ironically, the best control mechanism is the measurement of customer service satisfaction.

"Just Do It!"

Thank you Nike. You've got it right—"Just Do It!" This is what is so lacking in our society today and in today's managers and leaders in both the private and the public sectors. Where is the will to just get things done instead of convening endless studies, commissions, and meetings and not moving an inch without policies, procedures, and every bureaucratic piece of machinery imaginable? So many seem scared to death to make an informed and common sense decision. So many are so concerned about risk management and possible error or failure that they do nothing instead or engage in every bureaucratic CYA process possible. Results don't seem to matter as long as it can be shown that the politically, small p or large P, correct process has been followed.

What so many organizations desperately need today in both the private and public sectors are leaders and managers who can see and assess what needs to be done—what problems need fixing, what improvements can and should be made, and what goals can be achieved—and then go out and accomplish this by example and through the leadership of others. We need leaders and managers who have this kind of drive and enthusiasm and enjoy getting things done rather than following the politically correct process.

The process that does need to be paid attention to is that of good management i.e. creating a productive workplace culture where there is delegation of responsibility to all levels, the freedom to exercise initiative and to make informed common sense decisions, reward for performance and outcomes, and ongoing accountability of all concerned. This is far more effective risk management, by the way, than reams of policies and procedures, which no one reads in the first place or remembers if they did. Responsible, well informed, thinking employees who are allowed to make common sense decisions are the best line of defense for not only risk management, but also for quality control, customer service, and overall cost effectiveness. More policies and procedures accomplish nothing other than a focus on bureaucratic process rather than desired outcomes.

> **"Let judgement and personal conviction be important again. There is nothing unusual or frightening about it. Relying on ourselves is not, after all, a new ideology. It's just common sense."**
>
> —Philip K. Howard (1994, p.187)

Chapter X

REWARDS

"The greatest single obstacle to the success of today's organizations is the giant mismatch between the behavior we need and the behavior we reward."

—Michael LeBoeuf (1985, p.23)

The term "rewards" is used here to refer to all monetary compensation, all health and insurance benefits, all paid time off, and all other rewards, benefits, and perquisites, be they monetary or non-monetary that we receive from our employment.

Lack of alignment

Of all the people management practices that have been discussed in this book, rewards are probably the most frequently misaligned with the core principles of a productive workplace and the last to be changed. There are countless examples of hypocrisy in this area that we can read about everyday. The "golden parachutes" for incompetent executives, the enormous executive salaries despite poor organizational performance, the rollbacks to employee wages, but not to management's, and the greater percentage raises for management than for the employees, are just a few such examples. Regardless of how much attention is being paid in other areas to creating a participative workplace, those changes will not succeed if such contradictory messages regarding rewards are being sent to all employees; they are neither that stupid, nor that gullible.

One example of management hypocrisy in this area is found in the April 2004 issue of the magazine *Workforce Management*: "Two workers at a top U.S. airline came up with an idea that brought in $3 million in additional profits each year. When they were given a paltry $1,000 instead of the 10 percent reward to which they were entitled, they took the airline to court. The case reached the California Supreme Court—twice, no less—and directly involved the airline's CEO. The company ultimately abolished its suggestion program because of disputes over rewards." Unfortunately there are many companies out there that probably feel that the employees should consider themselves fortunate to have gotten even the $1,000 in the first place.

Traditional views

A lot of these practices are reflective of long held views regarding compensation and rewards in general:

- Managers deserve much more than employees; after all they are in charge, know more, and have more responsibility.
- Managers should be paid according to the number of employees they are responsible for.
- Managers are entitled to rewards for increased productivity, but not employees, because it is managers who are responsible for employee productivity.
- Managers are entitled to greater flexibility, as they are more responsible.
- Managers are entitled to various perquisites in recognition of their higher status and worth to the organization.

There is a long history of a sense of entitlement and self-interest that has, unfortunately, gone too far lately, as evidenced by so many examples today of corporate excess regarding management compensation.

The giant mismatch

The mismatch that Michael Le Boeuf (1985) refers to is not only a result of such traditional views, but also the result of many traditional pay practices that are based on outmoded management practices and concepts:

- Money and other extrinsic rewards are the prime means of motivation for greater productivity, greater sales, etc.
- Quality, customer service, and safety are not rewarded; productivity is.
- It is individual performance that matters most and must, therefore, be rewarded.
- If you make mistakes, they will be reflected on your performance evaluation and you will receive less of a raise.
- Pay is primarily based on seniority.
- There cannot be any flexibility in compensation plans in order to ensure equity.
- Compensation is a big dark secret that cannot be shared and must not even be discussed amongst employees.
- Profits are for owners and maybe shared with some managers, but not with employees.
- Pay is based on the job, not the incumbent.

These are just some of the prevalent pay practices that stand in the way of the productive behaviors that are required today on the part of employees at all levels in the organization. As Michael Le Boeuf (1985, p.23) says, the greatest management principle in the world is:

"The things that get rewarded get done."

It's the old adage, "You get what you pay for", and we've been paying for the wrong employee behaviors for a long time:

- We need employees who show initiative and creativity and who problem solve, yet we reward seniority and penalize employees for mistakes.

- We need to hire the best talent, yet we have rigid compensation policies that stipulate, for example, that you cannot hire above the midpoint of the salary range and you have to start at the bottom regarding the amount of vacation that you can expect.
- We need employees who take ownership, yet we won't give them any in the form of compensation.
- We need quality and customer service and safety, yet we reward productivity above all else and frequently to the exclusion of all else.
- We need teamwork, yet we assess and reward individual performance.
- We need employees to focus on the overall work rather than a narrowly defined job, yet we base compensation on the job.
- We need continuous improvement, yet we unnecessarily penalize employees for not following rigid policies and procedures.
- We need cross-functional thinking and cross-trained employees, yet we base compensation on the narrowly defined job.
- We say we value our employees, yet we still favor management with perquisites such as choice indoor parking spots, flexible time off, and additional benefits that are not available to employees.

Pay raises based on performance evaluation

One prevalent concept today, that merits individual attention, is that raises must be based on some form of performance evaluation and that only partial increases or none at all should be granted to those who are rated as substandard performers. There are several problems with this practice. Why do we retain substandard performers in the first place? Why are we, in effect, condoning poor performance by accepting it at all? What is being done to ensure that the employee performs at the desired level?

Withholding pay will do nothing to the performance of an employee who requires coaching and training or, failing that, requires placement in a position that they can perform well in, or termination. We have already seen that annual performance appraisal is a highly ineffective management practice; withholding pay increases based on such appraisal is equally ineffective. Employee performance and behavior must be dealt with separately outside of any compensation practice. If the employee is not performing up to the level desired, the answer is not to pay less, but to bring the employee's performance up to the required level.

Performance, of course, should be rewarded, but compensation is not an effective tool for influencing individual performance. If teamwork and ownership are desired behaviors today, then compensation should reflect team and organizational performance. Individual performance must be attended to through ongoing daily performance management.

Ownership

William Bridges (1994, p.162) says that,

> Two unrelated trends are further undermining the traditional salary. One is the shrinking of simple 'pay' and the expansion of shared earnings. The share can take the form of a bonus, stock options, or profit sharing, but in any form it de-emphasizes the job and emphasizes the work done and the contribution made. It also blurs the line, which jobs and salaries made very distinct, between the employee and the owner, and it does so with the intention of capturing from the employee the commitment felt only by someone with an ownership stake in a business.

The concept of greater sharing of rewards based on organizational performance, no matter what form the sharing takes, is somehow still viewed by many as a socialist tendency. From our point of view, sharing in the rewards is a logical extension of a capitalist philosophy, just as owning shares on the stock market is. It also makes good business sense as it favorably affects the bottom line. Such practices are not being promoted today purely because it's the right or ethical thing to do; they have a direct positive impact on overall productivity and the bottom line.

Open-book management

As mentioned earlier, there is a growing trend towards open-book management, where all employees are provided with all company information including all financials and they "have a direct stake in the company's success. If the business is profitable, they get a cut of the action. If it's not, they don't. In effect, open-book management teaches people to quit thinking of themselves as hired hands (with all that implies) and to start realizing that they are businesspeople (with all that implies). Their financial security depends on their joint success in the marketplace." (Case, 1995, p.38)

If you want employees to take ownership, then you have to give them ownership. This does not mean actual ownership of the company, but it does mean that employees must share in the fortunes of the company both for better and for worse. All other means of promoting ownership are a pretense and seen as such.

Pay for competencies, not the job

The second trend that William Bridges is referring to is that of paying for skills or overall competencies. He refers to an article by Milan Moravec and Robert Tucker (1992, pp.22-25) in which they point out that we cannot recognize or tap into the talents of individual employees until, "we change the way we design, allocate, and talk about work . . . . The focus should be on people's skills and behaviors, not on jobs." So many organizations talk quite sincerely about the need for productive employee behaviors, yet they continue to pay for the job.

> **"It is a truism that you get what you pay for, and with organizations needing to get new levels of effort and new degrees of flexibility from their workers, new kinds of compensation are going to become commonplace."**
>
> **—William Bridges (1994, p.163)**

Chapter XI

CHECK YOUR ALIGNMENT

**"The knee bone's connected to the thigh bone,
the thigh bone's connected to the . . ."**

The Paradox

The beginning of this book referred to the prevalent paradox in many of today's organizations. They try and create a more productive workplace where employees are intrinsically motivated to show initiative and creativity and provide excellent quality and customer service. Yet they retain many bureaucratic structures and systems of governance that inhibit such change and serve merely to create another flavor of the month. Table 2 from Chapter II shows some of those desired employee behaviors and the organizational practices that inhibit them:

TABLE 2
<u>ORGANIZATIONAL INHIBITORS</u>

Productive Behaviors	Organizational inhibitors
Customer service	Volume/cost focus
Focus on the *work*	Rigid, narrow *job* descriptions
Ownership	Lack of delegation
Teamwork	Focus on the individual

Knowledge and creativity	Rigid policies/rules
Initiative	Control orientation
Entrepreneurship	Paternal/authoritarian
Problem resolution	Multi-level hierarchy
Continuous improvement	Set, established methods
Cross-functional/multi-skilled	Functional specialization

These are, of course, only a few of many possible examples. One that has always remained with me stems from my former work as a Director of Human Resources for a major hospital. Although I was responsible for being the hospital's chief spokesman at the bargaining table with six unions, I was not allowed to claim for my parking fees at the hotel where the collective bargaining took place without an authorizing signature from my supervisor, the president. I could be responsible for the negotiations surrounding one payroll of over $30 million, yet I couldn't be trusted to claim for my own parking fees of only a few dollars! I had to waste my time and the president's in a useless and meaningless bureaucratic procedure. To get around this procedure, my secretary would claim the expenses as her own, I would sign for them, and then she would go to the Finance Department and receive the cash that she in turn would give to me. The irony is that all the staff in the Finance Department knew that this was a typical "work around", yet they knowingly complied as long as the proper paperwork was completed.

A system's perspective

It is critically important that one root out all such organizational practices; but what is even more important, however, is the understanding that all such inhibitors must be addressed at the same time. The organization must be viewed as one whole system with all parts interlocking and interrelated, rather than working at cross purposes with each other. It is only in this manner that we can avoid contradictory messages that disrupt and undermine any attempt at organizational and cultural change and result in another flavor of the month.

This view of the organization from the perspective of a single interrelated system is at the heart of the teachings of W. Edwards Deming (2000), commonly accepted as the father of quality management, and others such as Peter Scholtes (1998), who carried on the teachings of Dr. Deming. Systems thinking is also the focus of the best selling novel, *The Goal*, by Eliyahu Goldratt (1992). It is also at the heart of the concepts of lean manufacturing and lean enterprises in general. A *systems* view of an organization is not just a useful tool for a manufacturing or plant setting. It is not just an engineering tool; it is a point of view that should be applied to the entire organization.

What is alignment?

This is what is meant by alignment; all parts of the system or organization must be looked at to ensure that they are all aligned with the core principles of a productive workplace that were presented in the first two chapters of this book. It is not enough to merely create vision and mission statements that have such wonderful motherhood statements as, "Our employees are our greatest asset." or "We value quality and service above all." Too many organizations preach such lofty sentiments and goals and then go purchase the latest organizational change program in the hope that this will act as the silver bullet that changes their organizational culture and creates a more productive workplace. They want total quality management, but they will not relinquish control and assign responsibility to the individual employee. They want continuous improvement, but they will not relinquish all the bureaucratic rules and regulations, which stifle any creativity. Such misalignment sends contradictory messages, which negate the programs in question, create the latest flavor of the month, breed increasing cynicism and hypocrisy, and lead to even worse productivity.

As discussed in Chapter III, Frederick Herzberg (1969) spoke about job enrichment as a means of fostering the core principles of intrinsic motivation. He suggested that jobs be enriched and made more meaningful by removing some controls, delegating additional responsibility and increasing personal accountability. He also suggested that all employees be provided with timely performance information and complete units of work wherever possible. Also discussed was that most of these same recommendations have been made far more recently by Edward Lawler III (1986,1992). The point is, however, that none of these suggestions work successfully in isolation. You cannot relinquish control and delegate responsibility to the employee without providing all required information and feedback; to do so is setting people up for failure. You cannot increase personal accountability without delegating additional responsibility. All such management practices are interrelated and must be fully aligned.

The same need for alignment is true for the various people management practices that have been have presented in this book. None of these practices, for example, will have much chance of working well if the overall management style is not a participatory one. The traditional authoritarian or even paternalistic style of management, by its very nature, creates too many controls, a hierarchical structure, a lack of continuous learning and feedback, and other organizational inhibitors to a productive workplace.

To spend little time and effort in hiring new staff is self-defeating; yet many organizations take far too little time in ensuring a good fit with new hires. No amount of staff development and good performance management will be of much use unless you "hire right" in the first place.

On the other hand, spending the appropriate time and effort in hiring is completely negated if the organization does not provide the required orientation and ongoing training and coaching. No matter how good the new hires are, they will be set up for ultimate failure without the appropriate training and guidance. As a matter of fact, most of today's employees will probably leave first out of sheer frustration and in order to ensure their own successful career development. Good employees do not waste their time today by working for an organization that will not recognize and nurture their knowledge, talents, and initiative.

The same is true for performance management. No amount of performance feedback, positive or negative, is going to be successful if you don't hire the right employees in the first place and ensure that they receive the appropriate training. On the other hand, you will lose your good employees if you are not willing to deal with poor performance issues at all levels in the organization. Good employees will not tolerate a poor supervisor and will resent working alongside other employees who are incompetent or have a poor attitude. Termination of those that do not fit is a management practice that cannot be avoided if all parts of the system are to operate as effectively and efficiently as possible. No matter how well the other parts of the system work, if poor performers are not terminated, the good performers will view this as a clear sign that management is not really serious in their intentions to create and sustain a truly productive workplace.

> **"It is a wise man who said that there is no greater inequality than the equal treatment of unequals."**
>
> **—Felix Frankfurter**

The need for less hierarchy and a flat organizational structure is an area that is frequently neglected and, therefore, misaligned with other management practices. This is probably because a flat organizational structure has a very direct impact on management positions. It is far easier to talk about delegation of responsibility than it is to actually abolish unnecessary management positions. It is the same unfortunate attitude of self-preservation that we see so often in downsizing; employees, no matter how valuable, are easily laid off, while management positions, no matter how redundant, are usually left untouched. This hypocrisy does not go unnoticed and understandably breeds extreme cynicism. It is not enough to talk the talk; managers have to walk the talk if they expect results.

As far as the whole area of controls is concerned, we have already seen the example of my parking expenses. There are countless such examples in virtually all organizations. Restricted signing authorities, passwords for the photocopier, inability to access long distance on the phone, need to know controls on information, rigid job descriptions, policies for every conceivable eventuality, rigid vertical channels of communication, the list is endless. All such controls send contradictory messages to all employees; they imply that the employee cannot be trusted, they stifle initiative and creativity, and they stand in the way of quality, customer service, and continuous improvement. They also, as discussed in Chapter IX, do not provide true risk management; the best risk management is a well-trained and knowledgeable employee that is encouraged to use his or her informed discretion.

Rewards, as already mentioned, are probably the most often misaligned and again, as with organizational structure, the reason is that truly sharing the rewards with all employees directly affects management's own pocketbook and is against their own self-interests.

If the will to create a productive and participative workplace is sincerely there, then many of these practices will come naturally and evolve over time. They will need constant effort and attention. Mistakes will be made, but they will be rectified with the understanding and assistance of all staff at all levels.

The problem is the hypocritical approach that is so often the case, where there is no sincere will on the part of management to relinquish control and share rewards, for example. The hypocrisy and insincerity that is reflected in such misalignment will always show through and create, once again, another flavor of the month.

All the management practices that are required to create and sustain a truly productive workplace are interrelated and must be aligned with each other and the core principles of a productive workplace.

Chapter XII

QUANTITATIVE VERSUS QUALITATIVE

Peter Drucker once said, "What gets measured, gets managed." Today you cannot escape the prevalence of management metrics to measure all aspects of organizational as well as individual performance. KPIs or Key Performance Indicators include such measurements as CPO or cost per order, number of sales, number of defects, number of dissatisfied customers, and the list is virtually endless. Metrics specific to Human Resources are also prevalent and include such measurements as revenue per FTE (full-time equivalent), absenteeism rates, labor cost per FTE, turnover rates, and HR costs per FTE. User interfaces called "dashboards" are developed to present all this data in a way that is easy to read and comprehend.

Metrics a useful aid

According to businessdictionary.com, metrics are "standards of measurement by which efficiency, performance, progress, or quality of a plan, process, or product can be assessed." The use of such measurement tools is heavily emphasized in most schools of business and MBA programs. It is undoubtedly true that metrics are an extremely valuable tool in measuring both overall as well as specific performance, productivity, quality, and cost effectiveness. It is hard to understand why so many organizations and managers have not used metrics and how so many companies have survived without their extensive usage.

Reliance on metrics

But there is also a serious downside to this growing reliance on metrics. Managers are taught to rely on such measurements as they are supposedly more reliable, more objective, and fairer than any personal or qualitative analysis. They feel more comfortable in dealing with hard and cold measurements rather than any qualitative assessments. Metrics, in fact, are increasingly being used to the exclusion of any qualitative analysis, because it removes the aspect of personal judgement and assessment. Society in general reflects the same trend as individual values and opinions are called subjective and everything has to be backed up with quantitative statistics to be believed, no matter that these same statistics are developed, in many cases, by those with highly subjective viewpoints that they are trying to promote.

Metrics not a substitute
for judgement and discretion

It is so much easier to hide behind statistics rather than make and defend decisions based on your own personal judgement. In assessing someone's performance, for example, it is far easier to defend a poor evaluation and less than a full salary increase by telling an employee that they didn't score well enough on a quantitative evaluation system, than it is to explain and defend specifically what competencies need improving and why and to accept the responsibility of personally coaching his or her performance. Most issues of poor performance are not readily quantifiable, anyway, and are those, for example, of attitude, poor fit, lack of cooperation, and poor management style. As often stated throughout this book, it is a manager's prime responsibility to exercise their discretion and deal with performance issues. If they don't, then what are they managing?

What is also forgotten, is that the performance evaluation factors and the quantitative rating assigned to each factor must be based in the first place on someone's qualitative or subjective input; usually that of senior management and the Human Resources Department. It is impossible to avoid such qualitative input at some stage in any evaluation process. We cannot avoid the use of our own personal judgement—nor should we.

In assessing overall organizational effectiveness, "best practice" organizational reviews are based on a participative process where as many staff as possible are personally and confidentially interviewed. The main rationale for such a process is obvious. It is the employees who usually know best how the work should and can be done in the most cost effective and productive manner and, therefore, are most aware of what is impeding improvement and what needs to be changed. The internal or external consultants' job is to gather the input, to add their own generic expertise in organizational effectiveness and best practices, and to present the results in a coherent and meaningful manner with logical recommendations. Yet there are those who suggest that such analysis is based on biased opinions and that quantitative data from KPIs is more objective and fair. The selection of those KPIs, however, and the determination of what the acceptable quantifiable standards should be are based on qualitative or subjective input. What better way to review an organization's performance than to personally interview all staff and allow them to provide whatever input they feel is relevant and be able to probe where necessary to fully determine the why as well as the what? If the majority of such employee feedback identifies certain issues, is this not objective and quantifiable data?

Some even suggest that quantitative employee satisfaction and other surveys are a more objective means of reviewing organizational performance. Yet the metrics derived from such surveys won't show, for example, whether an organizational structure is efficient, whether departments need to be realigned, whether there is too much departmental turf protection with poor lateral communications, or whether management is ineffective. All of this requires face-to-face employee feedback with effective probing and qualitative analysis. The metrics may well be indicators to a trained observer or analyst, but then you still need to know the why and what to do to fix the issues, and metrics can't tell you that.

No amount of quantitative measurements is going to find out all the invaluable qualitative information, for example, that an "undercover boss" can discover. That is why good managers are constantly seeking and evaluating the feedback of all staff at all levels. They are constantly performing their own organizational reviews.

The choice of metrics is also of key importance in determining their usefulness. HR Metrics, for example, frequently include the percentage of completed performance evaluations as a measure of HR effectiveness. Yet traditional performance evaluations do not reflect best practice and have no bearing on the strategic relevance of HR to an organization. Health Care institutions are frequently using the metric of waiting times to be admitted to hospital and treatment as an indicator of their performance. Yet waiting times are primarily a reflection of staffing and budgets that are constantly manipulated for political reasons. Waiting times do little to reflect the actual effectiveness and efficiency of overall health care practices, procedures, and management.

Another example is ISO programs and their metrics, which measure standardization in production, but standardized excellence or mediocrity? Someone has to determine what the proper standards are and this again entails the use of judgement and discretion.

The excuse frequently made for the growing reliance on metrics is that they prevent the use of poor judgement on the part of some managers. If that's the case, then those managers should have their performance properly assessed and coached so that they can exercise better discretion in the future. More metrics are not a viable solution to the exercise of poor judgement.

Metrics don't tell you if you're at *maximum* possible productivity or *best* service. They can only tell you what the statistics are and whether or not you're meeting the goals that someone had to input in the first place based on their judgement and discretion. It is only through the input of all staff that one can determine whether or not maximum possible production has been reached; lean management, for example, demands employee participation to eliminate all wasted steps in any given process that do not add value.

Why choose an artificial metric performance goal in the first place? Why not just try and create a productive workplace culture where continuous improvement and quality are considered the norm?

Metrics can tell you *what* but not necessarily *why* or *how* to improve; it's employees who can provide the why and the how. Metrics are a highly useful aid to effective personal judgement and discretion, but they are not a replacement. This is why the core management principles that have been outlined in this book and which produce and foster a fully engaged and accountable work force are the most important elements in successful management. There is no effective alternative to a fully participative workplace with employees at all levels who are fully engaged and freely provide their ongoing input.

> "Away with the cant of 'Measures not men'!—the idle
> supposition that it is the harness and not the horses that
> draw the chariot along. If the comparison must be made,
> if the distinction must be taken, men are everything,
> measures comparatively nothing."
>
> George Canning—Speech to the House
> of Commons, 1801.

Chapter XIII

UNDERCOVER BOSS

No matter how much one may believe in and promote a participative workplace culture, it is the manager who is still in charge and ultimately responsible. But how can managers say that they are ultimately responsible and hold staff accountable, if they do not know what is actually going on in the organization? The larger the organization, the harder this becomes, but it is still possible.

Personal knowledge, not just performance data

You can't find out, however, by sitting behind a desk and staring at the latest corporate performance data on a computer screen. As stated earlier, effective managers spend a great deal of their time out of their offices and practice MBWA or Management By Walking Around. There is no better way of keeping your finger on the pulse of the organization than by roaming around, talking to people, and observing what goes on. Yes the performance data is important, but far more important is the actual human performance that drives this data. Do you know how your employees are actually performing? Do you know how good the service is that they provide? Do you know whether or not they actually like working for the organization and show the resultant initiative, productivity, and service? Do you know the most important question—how does the customer feel about your goods and services and how are they treated? Most of these questions are, of course, highly interrelated and interdependent. Most managers, however, do not have the answers and the corporate data does not always reflect the truth or predict future issues.

Some companies, for example, do not have much competition, so volume of sales and market share may not reflect the typically arrogant attitude towards customers and the generally poor customer service that pervades so many of these organizations. Do you know how customers are received when they call your company for information or service? Can they even get a human to respond? And if so, after how many minutes on hold and after how many different choices have to be entered for service, none of which really address your specific issue? Can you actually understand the customer representative who is all too often located in another country and does not understand you or your concern?

Do you know how easy or difficult it is to return a defective product to your company? Are you aware of the quality of your product or service? Do you even personally use them? Do you know firsthand how and under what conditions the product is made or is it made overseas in a plant that you have never visited? Do you know what impediments there are to productivity, quality, and service?

Are you also aware of what your employees have to go through every day in the performance of their duties? Are you aware of their working conditions, their total compensation package, and the daily pressures and difficulties that they face? Are you aware of how much impact they have on overall productivity and customer service and the quality of your goods and services?

The answers to many of the above questions reflect the basis on which your customers view your products, your service, and your overall organization. They do not rate you on the basis of your corporate statistics or even your market performance. But it is the actions of your employees and those of your customers that can dramatically change those statistics as well as market performance. It is critical, therefore, that you know how your employees are performing, whether or not they have the appropriate incentives, and what roadblocks stand in the way of how your customers are treated.

It is not a question of trust, but rather common sense.

The people who report to you may not even be aware of potential issues or, if they are, they may very well be reluctant to share them with you. You cannot totally rely on others to give you an accurate picture and you certainly cannot rely on anyone to give you what is even more important—a "feel" for the organization. Even in a fully participative workplace, that feel is critical, and you can only obtain that through first-hand experience. My partners and I find that, when called in to review the effectiveness and efficiency of an organization, we frequently obtain, through interviewing all employees, a better feel for the organization than the chief executive officer, and that the CEO is unaware of many issues that he or she is ultimately responsible for.

The manager is ultimately responsible.

The manager must develop this firsthand knowledge and understanding of the organization. You can only do that by personally visiting all areas of the organization, by informally talking to employees at all levels, and by seeing for yourself what exactly takes place on an ongoing basis. You need to call your own organization and ask a variety of typical questions to see what response and service you get. You need to ghost shop if you are running a retail enterprise. You need to visit your own website and see if the information or service that you require is available online. You need to call your own organization to see if you can actually contact someone in charge of a specific issue. And, yes, you need to use your own products and services.

You have the responsibility as a manager, let alone as the CEO, to know how your company is performing and you cannot do that by sitting in front of the computer and analyzing various statistics. This applies to all managers regardless of whether it is the private sector, the public sector, or a not for profit organization.

You will be a far more effective manager if you go see for yourself how things are running every now and then.

Chapter XIV

WHY MANAGERS GET FIRED

Technical competence

Managers, traditionally, have usually been selected and promoted on the basis of technical competence. The best engineer has been promoted to head the Engineering Department, the best accountant the Finance Department, and so forth. The same can be said for the chief executive officer in the private sector or the chief administrative officer in the public sector. The individual selected has usually been someone who is technically competent in at least one of the organization's main functions and someone who is familiar with all aspects of the organization as a whole; someone who "knows the industry" or someone who has "come up through the ranks."

There has been little if any emphasis on general organizational or people management competencies. The knowledge and ability, for example, of how to create a productive workplace where all employees are intrinsically motivated to take ownership and to be accountable for results has not been a required competency. This has not been necessary as the traditional management style has been to control the way people work; to control what they do, how they do it and every other aspect of their work. This has been the primary function of the manager. The people side of the business has been considered the soft side that really doesn't impact the bottom line as long as everyone does what they are told.

This traditional view of management competence is still, unfortunately, prevalent in many organizations. There is a growing recognition, however, that the only real and sustainable competitive advantage left is in human productivity and creating an organizational climate that supports and enhances it. As stated throughout this book, we need employees who take ownership of their work, who can problem solve, and who display initiative and creativity. Management's primary responsibility today, therefore, is to create and sustain such an organizational culture. This requires a far more democratic management style as well as different organizational structures and processes. As a result, managers today require more than just technical competence. This is equally true of the first line supervisor as it is of the chief executive officer.

Today's competencies

The main desired competencies for managers according to a generic management competency model outlined in *Competence at Work* by Lyle and Signe Spencer (1993, p.201) are:

- Impact and influence
- Achievement orientation
- Teamwork and cooperation
- Analytical thinking
- Initiative
- Developing others
- Self-confidence
- Directiveness / assertiveness
- Information seeking
- Team leadership
- Conceptual thinking

These are not purely technical competencies. These are competencies for managing people and the overall organization.

The U.S. National Association of Schools of Public Affairs and Administration (NASPAA) website says that, "Local government administrators must be integrative managers and administrators par excellence. Within the local government organization, they must provide staff leadership, design and implement change, . . . improve productivity, and set the tone for high standards of performance among staff."

Required competencies least taught

Everywhere we look we see the requirement for competencies in organizational effectiveness and design and in overall human resources management. Yet subjects in these areas are the least taught in most of our schools of business and our public administration educational programs. Schools of business still emphasize technical competence in the traditional areas of accounting, marketing, management information systems, business law and economics, for example. Programs in public administration still emphasize public legislation and finance. In addition, the few courses that are available in organizational effectiveness and human resources management are frequently electives and not part of the required core curriculum.

My partners and I mentor students from some of these academic programs. We are constantly shocked at the lack of knowledge that these students have been provided regarding productive management practices and the best current literature regarding these practices. Many of the relevant courses are also, unfortunately, taught by those with little actual work experience. It is interesting to note, that most of the best courses available that teach up-to-date management competencies are available through extension programs and continuing studies programs. Most of these courses, however, are only available to the mature working student; they are not offered as part of the normal degree or diploma programs.

Some of the academic experts in the field of management studies are also expressing their concerns based on some extensive research. The research of Jeffrey Pfeffer and Christina Fong (2002), that was referred to earlier, states that the MBA degree does not really serve any useful purpose. They conclude that the MBA degree does not produce more income or greater success in the business world and that the research done by the academic institutions involved has had little if any impact on day-to-day business practices. They state that there is little relevance of the typical business school curriculum to the competencies actually required to be successful in business. They refer to one study (Porter and McKibbin, 1988 p.65) in which many critics felt that quantitatively based analytical techniques received too much attention, while there was little attention given to developing leadership and interpersonal skills. Another study (Mintzberg and Gosling, 2002, p.28) noted that, "contemporary business education focuses on the functions of business more than the practice of managing."

The main reasons why managers get fired

Managers today must be able to create and sustain an organizational culture where employees take ownership of their work, problem solve, and display initiative and creativity. This requires, as shown throughout this book, a democratic style of management and a whole different set of competencies. It is the lack of such competencies that is the primary reason, in our experience, why managers get fired.

This is not about managers being fired because of a personality clash or difference of opinion with a new boss or a new board or council. That type of termination, fair or not, is an unfortunate, but ongoing part of corporate life. What are being discussed here are the main reasons that managers are legitimately, in our opinion, fired for poor performance.

The reasons listed below are, of course, highly interrelated, and where you find one, you are likely to find many of the others. All could be grouped, for example, under the heading of "Failure to create and sustain a productive organizational culture." Some separation of the reasons, however, has been provided so as to more clearly identify and discuss them.

Failure to deal with performance issues

There is one primary reason from our experience that stands out over all others and that is the failure to resolve staff performance issues. Ignoring poor performance, lack of fit or position redundancy does nothing to help the individual concerned or the organization and is by far the number one problem that we encounter as consultants. We are continually amazed at how many managers do not deal with performance issues. The reluctance is understandable as no one enjoys dealing with such issues, but the responsibility is a fundamental aspect of any manager's or leader's position. To be a manager requires that this responsibility be fully met at all times.

Creating and sustaining a productive organizational culture requires ongoing performance management. It requires constant care and attention to ensure that all employees fit the desired culture. It necessitates time and commitment in communicating organizational goals and requirements, discussing performance expectations, providing relevant feedback, training, and coaching and, in every manner possible, facilitating the optimum performance of all employees. It may also require discipline and termination. Managers who abdicate this responsibility fully deserve to be fired.

Failure to create a fully participative and productive workplace is another key reason for poor management performance. There are many aspects to this that have been discussed in preceding chapters:

- Delegating responsibility and accountability to the lowest possible level where the work is actually done.
- Creating a fully participative and responsible management team.
- Creating an organizational structure that supports the concept of a management team and eliminates all unnecessary hierarchical positions that are purely fulfilling an outmoded control function.
- Eliminating unnecessary policies, regulations, controls, and overall bureaucracy, which stand in the way of employee initiative, responsibility and accountability.
- Continuously looking for means to improve organizational performance. The first point in W. Edwards Deming's (2000, p.24) 14 Points for Management is to "Create a constancy of purpose toward improvement of product and service . . . ."

It is interesting to note that most of these practices are key components of all TQM programs and the concept of lean enterprises. Such programs may use different language, but the overall concepts and the desired results are the same.

Management's primary responsibility

Many managers will state that they don't have the time to do all of this; that they are too busy with their own work. This misses the point; it *is* their own work. It is management's primary responsibility to create a productive workplace culture so that the organization can strive for optimum performance. If they are too busy with technical duties such as accounting or engineering or sales or whatever their personal field of expertise is, the answer is to hire technical expertise in the required area. Managers who fail to understand what their true role is will inevitably fail in their performance and will get fired.

We are frequently challenged in our work as consultants to explain why a manager should be fired. Why can't they be properly trained or coached? Why can't they be simply told that they must change their management style? In most cases, unfortunately, the manager still believes and has been taught that his or her role is to control, to resolve all problems, and to be "in charge." This mind-set makes it very difficult for a manager to quickly adapt to an entirely different set of required competencies that are increasingly being demanded by today's participative and democratic workplaces. This takes time and, unfortunately for so many traditional managers, the time is not there nor the will or the ability in many cases.

The best for all concerned is for such managers to move on to a position for which they are far better qualified and where they do not adversely affect other employees, the organization as a whole, as well as their own career.

We desperately need competent managers in all sectors; managers who have the necessary competencies to provide the leadership required to create and sustain a participative and productive workplace, where quality and service are of paramount importance. It is so unfortunate and unfair that these competencies are still not the prime focus of our educational programs.

**We still all too often educate and hire managers
primarily for technical competence with the result that
they get fired for a lack of competence in leading people
and the organization.**

Chapter XV

GOOD MANAGEMENT IS LEADERSHIP

Throughout this book I have referred to managers and leaders without differentiation. It is fitting, therefore, to end with a discussion of leadership, which has, unfortunately, become the latest flavor of the month. Log on to Amazon.com and a search under books for "Organizational Leadership" will produce over 1500 listings, 215 with the actual word leadership in the title. Titles range from the bestselling *The Leadership Challenge* to other more esoteric titles such as *Transformational and Charismatic Leadership: The Road Ahead*, *Leadership Processes and Follower Self-Identity*, and *Identity is Destiny: Leadership and the Roots of Value Creation*.

Leadership in the business world used to be considered part and parcel of good management. The bestseller by Blanchard and Johnson (1983), *The One Minute Manager,* was followed by *Leadership and the One Minute Manager.* (Blanchard, Zigarmi, P. and Zigarmi, D., 1985) Being a good One Minute Manager was part and parcel of being a leader. Peter Scholtes (1998) described good leadership in terms of whole systems thinking and other aspects of management. Good management was considered good leadership and vice-versa.

Leadership distinct from management?

Now leadership is spoken of as a separate phenomenon, distinct from management. The buzzwords are vision, charisma, inspiration, credibility, encouragement, and values. Workshops purport to teach you these aspects of leadership as if the fundamentals of good management don't matter. What happened to the core management principles that this entire book is devoted to? These core management principles have been known for over half a century.

Teaching leadership as distinct from management is misleading and seriously detracts from the attention to the core management principles that are still, unfortunately, needed. As stated in previous chapters, the curricula of most Schools of Business are too narrowly focused on the traditionally taught business competencies such as accounting, marketing, and sales. Only recently, Henry Mintzberg (2004, p.5) in his latest book, *Managers Not MBAs*, says that, "It is time to recognize conventional MBA programs for what they are—or else close them down. They are specialized training in the functions of business, not general educating in the practice of managing . . . . It is time that our business schools gave proper attention to management."

Most of the fundamental aspects of leadership are exactly the same as those of good management and need to be recognized as such. In *The Leadership Challenge*, James Kouzes and Barry Posner (2008) talk about personal credibility and setting an example, clarifying values, fostering collaboration and teamwork, delegating responsibility, fostering accountability, setting clear standards, and recognizing performance. Surely this is precisely what we expect in a good manager today. Surely these are the same old core management principles restated in today's language. These are the same principles that are espoused by Edward Lawler III (1986,1992), Jeffery Pfeffer (1998), and others.

Why is it then that these competencies are referred to as leadership by some and as good management by so many others? Are they not one and the same? Is this not just another means of producing another "Silver Bullet"?

The other aspects of leadership that are so frequently mentioned are charisma and vision. Well some have them and some don't and they can't be taught. Not everyone is a JFK who can inspire an entire country by asking, "Ask not what your country can do for you, ask what you can do for your country." Not everyone has the incredible command of the English language as a Winston Churchill telling the people of England in World War II that, "Never in the field of human conflict was so much owed by so many to so few."

Both had charisma and vision, but just because you lack either one does not mean that you cannot be a good manager and, therefore, a good leader. Not everyone can be a Patton or a MacArthur, but remember that it was Eisenhower who was in charge of the Allied Forces and went on to be President.

The "leader" in leadership is not the charisma or the vision, it's the actual leading, of being out in front as in leading your troops in to battle or being personally on the scene at 9/11 as Rudolph Giuliani (2002) has described in his book, *Leadership*. The same is true for any good manager.

One cannot be a good manager without being a leader.

"Do as I say" as opposed to "do as I do", doesn't work in the workplace any better than it does at home. So managers must lead. They must clarify the values, provide the appropriate workplace culture, accept the overall responsibility, and be prepared to be held accountable. They must be out in front setting the personal example of such values as initiative, trust, honesty, ethics, participation, and teamwork. They must establish their personal credibility to lead. They must create the productive workplace that brings out the best in everyone including the collective vision.

Leaders, on the other hand, must be good managers.

Mintzberg (2004, p.6) says,

> …I use the words *management* and *leadership* interchangeably. It has become fashionable to distinguish them. Leadership is supposed to be something bigger, more important. I reject this distinction, simply because managers have to lead and leaders have to manage. Management without leadership is sterile; leadership without management is disconnected and encourages hubris. We should not be ceding management to leadership; in MBA programs or anywhere else.

To have a successful and productive organization of any kind it must be well managed. It is the leader's responsibility, therefore, to ensure that this occurs. The leader must put those management practices and principles into place that create a productive workplace, an effective government, or an efficient army. Leaders cannot do everything themselves and must, therefore, delegate responsibility to others.

This in turn means that they must be concerned with hiring the right people, with effectively managing performance, with recognizing achievement and dealing with poor performance, with training, with accountability and with openly providing information.

They must be fully trained and experienced in the core principles of good management and creating a productive workplace. You cannot be a leader without being a good manager. No amount of charisma or vision will compensate.

**Core management principles are just that;
they are *core principles*—core as in "a basic, essential,
or enduring part", and principle as in "a comprehensive
and fundamental law." It is far more productive,
and less time consuming, to concentrate on core
management principles, rather than looking for the
elusive Silver Bullet and continuously creating new
flavors of the month.**

REFERENCES

Blanchard, K. and Johnson, S., 1983. *The One Minute Manager.* New York: Berkley Books.

Blanchard, K. and Lorber, R., 1985. *Putting the One Minute Manager to Work.* New York: Berkley Books.

Blanchard, K., Zigarmi, P., and Zigarmi, D., 1985. *Leadership and the One Minute Manager.* New York: William Morrow and Company.

Blanchard, K., Carlos, J.P., and Randolph, A., 1996. *Empowerment Takes More Than a Minute.* San Francisco: Berrett-Koehler.

Block, P., 1993. *Stewardship.* San Francisco: Berrett-Koehler.

Bridges, W., 1994. *Job Shift.* Reading: Addison Wesley.

Case, J., 1995. *Open-Book Management.* New York: HarperBusiness.

Champy, J., 1996. *Reengineering Management.* New York: HarperBusiness.

Deming, W. Edwards, 2000. *Out of The Crisis.* Cambridge: MIT Press.

Farquhar, C.R. and Longair, J.A., 1966. *Creating High-Performance Organizations with People.* Ottawa: The Conference Board of Canada.

Giuliani, R.W., 2002. *Leadership.* New York: Hyperion.

Goldratt, E. M. and Cox, J., 1992. *The Goal.* Great Barrington: North River Press.

Goold, M. and Campbell, A., 2002. *Designing Effective Organizations.* San Francisco: Jossey-Bass.

Hamel, G. and Prahalad, C.K., 1989. Strategic Intent. *Harvard Business Review*, May-June.

Hammer, M., 1993. The Future of Middle Managers. *Management Review.*

Herzberg, F., 1966. *Work and the Nature of Man.* New York: Thomas Y. Crowell.

Howard, P.K., 1994. *The Death of Common Sense.* New York: Warner Books.

Kouzes, J.M. and Posner, B.Z., 2008. *The Leadership Challenge.* San Francisco: Jossey-Bass.

Lawler III, E.E., 1992. *The Ultimate Advantage: Creating the High-Involvement Organization.* San Francisco: Jossey-Bass.

Lawler III, E.E., 1986. *High-Involvement Management.* San Francisco: Jossey-Bass.

LeBoeuf, M., 1985. *The Greatest Management Principle In The World.* New York: G.P. Putnam's Sons.

Marrow, A.J., 1969. *The Practical Theorist: The Life and Work of Kurt Lewin.* New York: Basic.

Maslow, A., 1987. *Motivation and Personality.* New York: HarperCollins.

McGregor, D., 1960. *The Human Side of Enterprise.* New York: McGraw-Hill.

Mintzberg, H., 2004. *Managers Not MBAs.* San Francisco: Berrett-Koehler.

Mintzberg, H., 2002. Reality programming for MBAs. *Strategy and Business,* 26(1), pp.28-31.

Moravec, M. and Tucker, R., 1992. Job Descriptions for the 21st Century. *Personnel Journal,* June.

Peters, T. and Austin, N., 1985. *A Passion For Excellence.* New York: Warner Books.

Pfeffer, J., 1998. *The Human Equation.* Boston: Harvard Business School Press.

Pfeffer, J. and Fong, C.T., 2002. The End of Business Schools? Less Success Than Meets The Eye. *Academy of Management Learning and Education,* Volume I.

Pojidaeff, D., 1995. The Core Principles of Participative Management. The *Journal for Quality and Participation,* 18(7) December.

Porter, L.W. and McKibbin, L.E., 1988. *Management Education and Development.* New York: McGraw-Hill.

Scholtes, P.R., 1998. *The Leader's Handbook.* New York: McGraw-Hill.

Semler, R., 1993. *Maverick.* New York: Warner Books.

Senge, P., 1990. *The Fifth Discipline.* New York: Currency Doubleday.

Senge, P., 1992. Building Learning Organizations. The *Journal For Quality and Participation,* 15(2) March.

Spencer, L.M. and Spencer, S.M., 1993. *Competence at Work.* New York: John Wiley & Sons, Inc.

ABOUT THE AUTHOR

Dimitri Pojidaeff is a Partner in HR Group Management Consultants who have specialized in organizational effectiveness and human resources management since 1993. They also provide a 1-800 Human Resources Line to the members of several public and private associations for advice and assistance in these areas, as well as publish a newsletter on best practices.

A graduate of Phillips Academy—Andover, Columbia University, and the Banff School of Management, Pojidaeff has broad training in Human Resources Management, Organization and Staff Development, and Employee Relations. He has developed and presented management development seminars on such topics as Effective Communication Skills, Recruitment and Selection, Performance Management, and Participative Workplaces and has taught University credit courses in such subjects as Human Relations in Business, Organizational Behavior, and Human Resources Management. He has also published several articles on organizational effectiveness.

He has been a senior human resources executive and consultant for several large organizations across Canada and has extensive experience in all areas of organizational effectiveness, human resources management, and employee relations. Pojidaeff offers his clients first-hand experience and expertise in what works, what doesn't and why, and what organizational change is required to effect and sustain participative and productive workplaces. His consulting practice involves assisting organizations to become more productive through organizational and human resource management practices that create a more participative, productive, and cost effective workplace. He has reviewed and improved the effectiveness of numerous private and public organizations and has established and restructured Human Resources departments for several large organizations across Canada.

He is committed to the concept that true continuing productivity is only sustained when employees at all levels have both responsibility and accountability for the work that they do and its outcome.